8/6/91

Loved one —

I have always been or ... through ... Love.

Help Me Make It Through the Day

Phil. 1:3

HELP ME
Make It Through the Day

Luther Joe Thompson

BROADMAN PRESS
Nashville, Tennessee

© Copyright 1989 ● Broadman Press
All rights reserved
4250-52
ISBN: 0-8054-5052-1
Dewey Decimal Classification: 248.4
Subject Heading: CHRISTIAN LIFE
Library of Congress Catalog Number: 88-19825
Printed in the United States of America

Unless otherwise stated, all Scripture quotations are from the King James Version of the Bible. Scripture quotations marked NIV are from HOLY BIBLE *New International Version,* copyright © 1978, New York Bible Society. Used by permission. Scripture quotations marked RSV are from the Revised Standard Version of the Bible, copyrighted 1946, 1952, © 1971, 1973.

Scripture quotations marked Moffatt are from *The Bible: a New Translation* by James A. R. Moffatt. Copyright © 1935 by Harper and Row, Publishers, Inc. Used by permission.

Scripture quotations marked NEB are from *The New English Bible.* Copyright © The Delegates of the Oxford University Press and the Syndics of the Cambridge University Press, 1961, 1970. Reprinted by permission.

Library of Congress Cataloging-in-Publication Data

Thompson, Luther Joe.
  Help me make it through the day / Luther Joe Thompson.
    p. cm.
  ISBN 0-8054-5052-1
  1. Christian life I. Title.
BV4501.2.T489 1989
248.4'86132—dc19   88-19825
                                                                  CIP

To my siblings:
Virginia, Jack, and Carolyn
Who have helped me make it through my days.

Contents

Contents

Preface

Help Me Make It Through the Day began a long time ago. Maybe it began with my sense of wanting to help others, an impulse which both attracted and frightened me. Or perhaps it began in my childhood home.

I am not sure when I began to feel with and for people in trouble and need—or when I wanted to reach out and help. As I grew older and matured in my career, the concerns of this book multiplied. I soon discovered that wanting to help was not the same as helping. I found that real love could be costly, demanding, painful, incessant, and that even when we do our best, there may be very little evidence that we have helped. I've somehow learned the difference between "the needs people feel they have" and "the needs I think they should have." We can't help people unless and until we come to respect and honor their rights as individuals—their autonomy.

A caring, feeling book store manager remarked to me, "The customers come in all the time asking for books to help them make it through the day. Their needs are varied, but their cry is always the same: 'My son is hooked on drugs.' 'My daughter is living with a man who's using her.' 'My teenager has left home, and I don't know where she is.' 'My marriage is on the rocks.' 'Why can't I get along with other people?' 'My husband is depressed.' 'I sometimes think I'll go crazy.' 'I can't live with myself.' On and on they go. If someone will write a book for them, they'll buy it."

As the years have passed I have learned a little about meeting human need. We *can't* meet the other person's need. All we can do is love them and point them to the source of healing and power. We're neither good enough nor wise enough to know what is best for them, let alone change or heal them. Yet the resiliency and idealism of the human spirit are incredible.

A mother sent her small daughter to make a purchase at the neighborhood store. The girl was gone so long the mother became concerned about her, and she asked for an explanation when the child finally came back. "On my way home I passed Mary's house. She broke her doll, and I stopped to help her."

"What in the world could you do to help?" her mother asked.

"Oh, I sat down and helped her cry."

Sometimes this is all we can do, and we must be willing to do it if we want to help others help themselves. In this book I will try to speak "the truth in love."

Maybe you wonder how I determined the series of human problems to be addressed in this book. I have tried to hear the problems people feel they have, not the ones I think they should have. There can be a difference. I have tried to hear these problems with an understanding kind of love.

Surveys were made and respondees' opinions were carefully considered. In one survey, under the title: *Dealing with Feelings of Desperation,* 270 individuals responded. Eighteen percent said they experienced such feelings once a week, 37 percent once a month and 12 percent not at all. (The word *desperation* may have been too strong.) In answer to the question: *Which of the following cause you problems?* Fifty-six percent said stress, 46 percent anxiety, 24 percent hurt feelings, 23 percent loneliness, 22 percent bad habits, guilt, anger, and lack of motivation tied at 21 percent, and children came in at 20 percent. While there was considerable variety among responders in economic and social status, they were predominately middle-class American people.

Numerous significant notations were made on the survey forms: "Why can't I tell someone about my real hurts?" "I wanted to die." "I felt like I was caught in a vice with somebody tightening the screws." "Don't tell me what I ought to do; I can't!" "I wondered if anyone cared." And hundreds more! The problems chosen represent the challenges we face as human beings.

In writing this book, I've wondered at my presumption, being neither a psychiatrist nor specialist in human behavior, in undertaking such a venture. I suppose, my excuse is my concern for people in their needs. Neither academic nor technical, this book is intended to be practical. In addition, there is the problem of giving sufficient credit where credit is due. I'm indebted to many people for ideas and insights which long ago became so much a part of my thinking that I no longer remember their source. Any lack of acknowledgement of credit is unintentional.

Let me express my special thanks to my seminary colleagues, my wife, and my Garrett Fellow, William Pyle, who have been of incomparable assistance in this project.

If this book helps you make it through your day, that will "make my day"!

Luther Joe Thompson
Shelbyville, Kentucky

1 One Day at a Time
Making It Through the Day

Now is the only time we own;
Love life, toil with a will;
Do not wait until tomorrow,
    for the clock may then be still.
                          —Will Rogers

A bird of considerable dignity and independence sat on
a perch at the door of the hunting lodge, and as hunters
entered, he'd give his only speech: "One at a time, gentlemen, one at a time, please!" No one knew where he learned
it, but it was written indelibly on whatever brain he had.
The hunters loved him and were upset when he disappeared. After days of searching, they found him in a hor-
nets' nest, nearly done for, but still giving his speech: "One
at a time, gentlemen, one at a time, please!" His logic was
good, but his circumstances were horrible. How do we live
one day at a time?

We know we should, but it's one thing to believe "This
is the day the Lord hath made" and another to "rejoice
and be glad in it". There are "hornet days" and "South-
Sea-Island days," and each has its music and song. There

is no doubt a common key, but it requires a special musical ear to detect it.

A lovely lady often called me early in the morning to request "a word to help me make it through the day." She was elderly and ill, living all alone and struggling with cancer, and she was a sensitive, intelligent woman of faith. I'd think for a moment, perhaps consult my Bible, and then read her a text. "Thank you," she'd reply and be gone.

"Help me make it through the day!" When we love people, we often hear that cry. Some are desperate, some defeated, some scared and running, some confused, and some depressed. The list is nearly endless: the bewildered teenager, the desperate parent, the lonely old people, the spouse with a marriage on the brink, the anxious, the guilt ridden, and the cynical. Tedium, ennui, anxiety, frustration, depression—too often these are emotions that defeat the human spirit and rob us of usefulness and joy.

> We live in deeds, not years; in thoughts, not breath;
> In feelings, not in figures on a dial.
> We should count time by heart-throbs. He most lives
> Who thinks most, feels noblest, acts best.[1]

We agree with the poet; yet we know his wisdom is partial and incomplete. We not only live in deeds but also in days. Our thoughts, feelings, and actions have no reality apart from our experience of time. All of us live day by day, and time is life. I am what I do with my time. For most of us, our time is our days. "This Being of mine," wrote Marcus Aurelius long ago, "whatever it really is, consists of a little flesh, a little breath, and the part which governs."[2] Would that astonishing pagan philosopher and

---

Roman emperor agree that "the part which governs" is what we call "the soul," the image of God within us? I'm not certain, yet I know that even "the part which governs," however we may define it, can only guide us in the use of our days upon this planet. By the use of our days we translate H. T. Leslie's epigram into fact: "The game of life is not so much in holding a good hand as in playing a poor one well."

In the most remarkable ways, we live by days, not hours, weeks, months, or years. A month is too long, an hour too short. Our days are the building blocks of our lives as we stack them, one on top of another, until one day the building is complete. Isn't it true that the essential difference between how people live is in the way they use their day? We may dream, speculate, plan by years, decades, even centuries, but we act by days.

Here is the question of questions for most of us. If I can win this day, if I can make it useful and worthwhile, if I can endure it without loss—then I am en route to building a better life. Good lives are built, not by grand plans, elevated dreams, or dramatic aspirations, but by living well one day at a time. If I can make it through this day, without loss and perhaps with some tangible gain, then I'm on target. "Help me make it through the day" is more than a prayer. It's a plan.

Here is a truth which permeates ancient literature, especially the Bible of the Jews and Christians. The whole concept of creation in Genesis, its first book, is set in the framework of God's days. We are told that even God worked and rested, moving in patterned sequence and harmony. "The day of the Lord" is an Old Testament idea that filled the mind of the ancient Jew.

How do we assume control of our lives? Really, there is only one way: by taking control of our days. How do we do that? Do you recall the line from the song that says you can't see daylight until you make it through the night? Yet there is also the matter of making it through the day once you see the dawn. Sometimes it seems easier to endure the tedium of the night than to utilize the trauma of the day. We partly make it through the day by being honest about the variety of days all of us must endure. There are days of pleasure, excitement, surprise, fulfillment, and promise. These are days to be claimed, enjoyed, savored, and remembered. But there are also days of pressure, pain, terror, bewilderment, tedium, weariness, confusion, days when we protest, "This is not my day!" What has been your worst day? Your best? Remember "the best," and be thankful you made it through "the worst."

First, we are not asking how to make it through the week or the month or the year—just how to make it through the day, indeed through this day. A moment ago I asked you to think about your worst day. Now in retrospect, what counsel would you give yourself and others who are going through tough times? Expect resentment, anger, and frustration? Sooner or later those emotions come. When we're in pain, we tend to regress. The infant in us comes out. Terror can bring out the latent violence within us. Perhaps we expect too much of ourselves and should be grateful for simple endurance.

Second, we must make the most of our good days. In fact, we must make the most of the good in every day. Positive reinforcement is more profitable than negative recrimination. We are told that every morning when Henry David Thoreau awakened, he would lie in bed for a few moments and review all the good things about himself he could remember: his good health, his material abundance, his friends, his loved ones, his prospects for the day, and the interesting things he had to do. He felt it added luster to his day.

Celebrate life's joys. Savor your good days. Treasure them. Store them in the choicest rooms of your memory. Place them on ready recall. Share them often. Capitalize on them.

Third, determine in advance, whatever a day may bring, that you will reject the negative response. When trouble comes, the agony is too severe to make that choice after you are submerged in it. All of us react to pressure, pain, and difficulty in a variety of ways. We can resent it or complain about it, deny it or drug it. As an honest friend of mine put it, "When it really gets rough, I always get tanked." And he confessed, "Of course, all that does is compound my trouble." There are days that bring such terrible news, reflect such pain, chagrin, and anguish that the first reaction is a feeling of revulsion that tempts us to deny the reality we face. But denying misery doesn't make it go away.

There is another reaction even more dangerous than trying to deny reality, and that relates to the person who permits his life to grow sour, loads himself with guilt, and then begins the brutalizing process of punishing himself. His inverted anger becomes a seedbed for depression, and he multiplies his troubles and seems to wallow in his misery. Be honest about your faults; confess your sins but don't deprecate yourself. To do so brings only misery and pain. You were not made in God's image to put yourself down. If God loves you, try to love yourself, even on your bad days.

Determine in advance how you will react. Accept the fact of your humanity. Don't expect perfection. Remind yourself that you are both good and bad. If you ask Him, God forgives you; learn to forgive yourself. Avoid self-pity like the plague. You don't have to rationalize pain to tolerate it. Find friends with whom you can share your troubles. Sometimes a sense of humor can reduce pressure, but more often it hurts too much to laugh, and sometimes it doesn't do much good to cry. But determine your strategy in advance and don't expect the impossible.

Fourth, it's better to work it out than to sigh it out. There is a lovely story of a young woman who had a beautiful voice, but she would never subject herself to the routine necessary to use her talent in the church choir. Then there came a day when her husband was drafted for military service. Immediately she reported to choir rehearsal, and when someone asked for an explanation, she replied, "I decided to sing it out rather than sigh it out." Activity may be the healthiest diversion of all.

Yet, ironically, sometimes when the deepest anguish comes we are not even able to work. Then all we have left is to commit the activities of our minds to the positive, the helpful, and the good. This is not only the best way—it is the only way. We don't dip darkness out of a room with a teaspoon or even a five-gallon bucket—we raise the blinds. When we open our minds and hearts to God's love, there is little room left for evil. E. Stanley Jones said, "You are far more likely to act yourself out of a bad way of thinking than to think yourself out of a bad way of acting."

Fifth, see every day as one with eternal significance. Perhaps you are reading this book in the hopes of making it through the day—and then being able to tackle the night. You may—or may not—have a religious orientation. I set out to write this book for those who are religious and those who are maybe not so religious.

Personally, I do like to surround myself with watchwords and slogans. One of mine is quite religious. I call it my "morning waker-upper." "This is the day which the Lord hath made; we will rejoice and be glad in it." For me, there are days—when apart from my conviction that a Supreme Being made them—that would contain only doom and gloom. Sometimes it appears the devil made those days. And isn't it strange how many people seem to believe in the devil but don't believe in God?

In the end, happiness is a matter of choice. For me the choice is based on faith in God. This day is my moment of truth, my time of reality, my opportunity to merge time with eternity.

Why do so many of us live either in the past or in the future? This point in time is the only real moment I will ever know. I can reject it, or I can claim it, endure it, and even rejoice in it.

We live in a world of time and space, of biological fact and personal choice, of emotions we either experience and utilize or ignore and find costly and damaging. How do we deal with fear, anxiety, grief, frustration, loathing, anger, and boredom? Our choices are limited. We can learn to capitalize on them, see them as the driving forces of life, learn to tolerate them—and perhaps even enjoy them—or let them fill us with frustration and pain, maybe ultimately destroying us.

Yes, you can make it through the day! That's what this book is all about. Put worry to work for you. Let anger energize you. Make stress your friend. Let grief be your teacher. Use laughter for healing. You will not only survive, but you will have a lot of fun, and your friends will be glad you're alive.

Suggestions for Making It Through the Day

1. *Be glad you've survived.*
2. *Remember that all troubles pass.*
3. *Major on your assets.*
4. *Be as happy as you can.*

2 How to Live with "Impossible" People
Personal Relationships

"It was said of Patrick Henry that he kept other people awake all night."

"You married him. I didn't! I know he's my daddy, but I never would have picked him!" The explosion came from a teenager protesting to her mother in a department store. Unfortunately or fortunately as circumstances might warrant, I could not hear the mother's reply. I'm not really given to eavesdropping, but I recall other teenagers angrily declaring about their parents, "They're killing me!" and I wanted to whisper, "Parents have no monopoly on murder." A small boy got in a fight with a neighbor boy, and his mother, discovering the altercation, punished him. Through his tears, he rationalized, "I'd be OK if it weren't for folks!"

Relationships have been called "the essence of living," and all human beings long for intimacy with other human beings, yet satisfying intimacy can be an elusive and fragile commodity. Do you ever wonder why certain people are able to draw others to them and gain their admiration and affection, but others have a way of repulsing people? Relationships have to do with friendships, for friendship is the springboard to love. Can you make friends, keep friends, and enjoy friends?

Alan Loy McGinnis in his delightful book *The Friendship Factor* gives down-to-earth suggestions for making and keeping friendships:

1. Assign priority to your relationships.
2. Cultivate transparency.
3. Communicate warmth.
4. Learn the gestures of love.
5. Create space in your relationships.
6. Don't be afraid of touch.
7. Be liberal with praise.
8. Learn to listen.
9. Locate the trouble spot.
10. Be the first to bury the hatchet.[1]

But you say, "My problem is not with the people I want as friends but with those with whom I must work, live, or associate whom I don't like." You refer to a superior or someone who works in your office or on your shift or who supervises your work, someone from whom there is no escape, and they're giving you ulcers or migraine or something else. Again, maybe they are people you love: a spouse, a sibling, a parent, or a child. You do care for them but they have a way of driving you up a wall.

Once as an overnight guest in the home of a relative, I found an intriguing book on a bedside table: *How to Make Yourself Miserable* by Dan Greenberg. First the book dealt with how to drive yourself up a wall, then how to drive others up a wall. You see, the possibilities are almost endless, and that night before dropping off to sleep I jotted down some things to consider the next day:

- Misery is 90 percent self-inflicted.
- The primary factor in what you get out of life is you.
- It's more fun blaming others, but more futile.
- All marriages are happy; the rub comes in living together.
- Everybody loves to give advice; nobody wants to take it.
- Nearly all good things come by choice.

Let me assure you, the next morning I was positive at the breakfast table.

Living with impossible people! What does that bring to mind? A boss who is arbitrary, overbearing, and unfair? A husband or wife, who in the name of love, is manipulative, domineering, and dogmatic? A child, who try as you may, will not respond to your love?

There are impossible clergy. Does it surprise you I'd confess it? God has no perfect representatives, and for that matter, what would church members do with perfect ministers if they had them? Do you recall the story of the church member who came out of the tavern drunk? "Oh, Padre," he said, "I'm so sorry for you to see me drunk!" "But God sees you," the pastor replied. "Oh, I know," responded the inebriated man. "But He's no blabbermouth."[2]

How easily we pontificate, give advice, criticize, and, all the while, imagine we're being friends. Impossible people increase pain rather than lessen it. There are so many ways to help. Love is ingenious, creative, and imaginative. I remember so vividly, long ago while I was still an unmarried pastor, a member coming at the end of worship, gently teasing me about my flashy tie. Then with a twinkle in her eye, she told me if I'd surrender my tie to her, so I could never wear it again, she'd give me a half-dozen new ties in exchange. Smiling she pulled a box of ties out of her coat. I looked the ties over, took mine off, and made the exchange. Incidentally, the lady had a point. My flock needed a minister who'd wear more appropriate ties. But the amazing thing was how she did it. Sugar does help the medicine go down.

We live in an imperfect world, associate with imperfect people, and have faults and foibles ourselves. To build and maintain satisfying relationships we need a healthy realism and a full measure of personal candor and honesty. We must accept the fact that there are indeed impossible people, and at times all of us can be impossible. The "everybody's-wonderful" syndrome solves nothing and often makes the relationship more difficult. The new groom has a smoother adjustment to posthoneymoon reality if he accepted his beloved's imperfections before the wedding.

Was there ever a teenager who at some time did not feel her parents were driving her crazy? The strange feeling is normal for the youngster who is struggling to find her own adulthood. Love her and she may soon change. The impossible quality within us may be a stage in our development, or it may represent a fixation at some stage of immaturity or even a character flaw. The more objective and honest we are about these facts of human relationships, the sooner we learn to tolerate and make the necessary adjustments.

We must learn to tolerate differences, work at communication, develop patience and sensitivity, and exercise our sense of humor. This is a lifelong process. To neglect

it is to guarantee grief and pain both for others and ourselves. Sometimes our only recourse is to sever relationships. There are divorces that are inevitable, even children
who must find relief from parental pressure. Sometimes
jobs must be changed. It is in the context of such problems
that love is so necessary and so powerful. Yet love does not
necessarily mean relationships can never be severed.

"What do you do with people who make you feel that
way?" The question came from a sensitive, deeply religious friend who was committed to living by the law of
love, and had to do with a longtime relationship which
expressed as much hate as love. Actually, her "so-called
friend" seemed to bring her more pain than pleasure.

In my own experience, I have concluded that there are
people, who for the health of both of us, we must give each
other room. Now I don't recommend this, but in a limited
number of instances I have found it my only satisfactory
solution. Perhaps you feel such a reaction contrary to love;
yet love cannot be forced, and certainly not upon someone
else. When this seems necessary, I make a special effort to
see there is no hate or anger involved, simply a matter of
avoiding friction. We once had a friend who seemed unable to avoid a "so-called friend" who was forever doing
her in, yet she would continue the relationship. To press
damaging relationships can multiply misery. To be adult
is to admit no person can win them all.

When I have dealt with such situations as best I can, I
try to put it out of mind until some new and better opportunity arises where the relationship can be improved. I
don't brood over it or allow it to generate guilt or hostility
in me. I try to understand people who seem impossible to
me, learn from them if I can, and refuse to feel hostile

toward them. Finally, I try to put them in what I call a Romans 8:28 context, that is with God's help remember "all things work together for good to them that love God." And always I work at improving my sense of humor. My impossibilities seem less anguishing when I can laugh at them.

Above all, when it comes to dealing with impossible people, nothing is so important as having *a strategy of love.* However let me warn you, love can be demanding and costly. Perhaps no test of our love is so severe as our relation to impossible people. Here we put our faith on the line, prove it valid or invalid.

Here is a five-part strategy of love:

A strategy of love rules out hate, hostility, and anger as possibilities in responding to impossible people. This is the place to start. No man can hate and love at the same time. Our Lord died for those who rejected Him, hated Him, despised Him, even crucified Him, and it is that kind of love which makes reconciliation possible.

Learn to handle anger constructively. Anger is perhaps the most expected and damaging response when we are threatened in our most intimate and treasured relationships. An executive who is a pattern of rectitude in his office may become a tyrant when challenged at home. In the office, he is privileged, powerful, and esteemed; at home he is just another member of a family who must earn trust and prove his love. If one wishes to live by the law of love, one must find constructive ways to handle anger. You can talk it out, work it off, or find a friend who can help you ventilate it. As marriage therapists tell us, even fighting can be done constructively if participants agree on rules and limitations, select an appropriate time, stick to the subject, refuse to dredge up past faults, and major on solutions rather than assigning blame.

If we are to build community, love says we must admit our faults and work at overcoming them. How often I see a person as impossible because of some hidden fault in me. I dislike the person who reminds me of something I dislike about myself. So much of my criticism is vicarious self-criticism. A lot of the impossible in other people lies within me. Why do some people generate so much hostility in me? When I answer that I will have gone a long way toward making the impossible person possible for me.

Love develops a sense of humor. "Love is what you have been through together," a mother of twelve said. "You laugh and cry and laugh again, and the more you laugh, the better." Is that the reason marriage and romance have been defined as "one crazy thing after another"? All who have a happy, healthy family life understand what it means to sit down, laugh, cry, and laugh again. Perhaps laughter is the closest thing to prayer in human relationships.

Finally, love takes us back to the cross where we learn to love and to live. We used to sing at church, "At the cross, at the cross where I first saw the light," but at the cross we see more than that: we see God's love for us, the power of love to redeem, and the key to building love into our human relationships.

Five Things to Remember

1. *Win them all if you can; friendship is life's elixir.*
2. *If some persons seem impossible, remember the impossibility may be in you.*
3. *Resolve to love even if you can't like.*

4. *Think positively and act lovingly. Miracles still happen.*
5. *Pray daily for all the impossible people you know, including yourself.*

3   Laughing Your Way to Health
A Sense of Humor

"There is no cure for birth and death save to enjoy the interval."

—George Santayana

If you were to telephone me, reporting an excruciating headache, a sleepless night and a hundred-degree fever, and I advised you to sit down and laugh it off, how would you react? Would you assume I was off my rocker or downright sadistic? I could understand if you did.

Yet there can be healing in a sense of humor. Often the difference between survival and nonsurvival for human beings lies in such things as finding meaning and purpose in one's suffering, nearness to those who love us, a healthy faith in God, and, interestingly enough, possessing a sense of humor. If I had my time to go over, I'd resolve to laugh myself out of trouble more often. Laughter as a choice can contribute to health. I can choose "the medicine of a merry heart" even when its logic evades me. One way to make it through the day is to cultivate mirth, develop a sense of humor, learn to laugh at yourself, with yourself, and to yourself. As funny as it may seem, and as incongruous, you can laugh yourself to health.

"Often, my grandmother felt bad, especially in the morning. She found it difficult to get up. My grandfather, aware of this, sometimes would suggest a trip for the day. Immediately, grandmother's feelings would improve, and by the hour for the trip, she would be in perfect health." That's the way my friend described it.

Grandmother's feelings were not merely in her mind. She suffered from low blood pressure. The anticipated joy of a trip actually improved her bodily functions.

Have you ever thought of laughter as a medicine for health? Ironically, many have not. The best gifts we either take for granted or spurn. Here is one of life's strange ironies. How long has it been since you thought it important to thank God for a sense of humor?

Laughter has been called "the tranquilizer with no side effects," yet few consider it significant or purposefully try to develop it. How often do you take exercises in laughter? Do you see it as necessary as prayer, indeed a kind of prayer? William Thackeray contended, "A good laugh is sunshine in the house." Martin Luther in typical fashion declared, "If you're not allowed to laugh in heaven, I don't want to go there." And the Roman philosopher Seneca said, "It better befits a man to laugh at life than to lament over it."

He had a twinkle in his eye, a smile on his lips, a mischievous sort of grin on his face. He always seemed happy. Indeed he was one of the more pleasant men I have known. He's been gone almost a quarter of a century, but his memory is as vivid as if it were yesterday.

He knew more funny stories, more ways to encourage you when you were down, more devices to make you laugh

when you felt like crying than any other person I have
every met. He could remember more good things about
more people, and how he loved to tell them! To see him
walk in a room, especially when you were tired or depressed, was to see the sunshine come out.

Yet he was not handsome or talented, not striking or
famous, not brilliant or scintillating. He knew this and
often made it the center of his humor. But he had a gift
for happiness, he was a dispenser of "a merry heart."
Every time I saw him, I thought of that ancient proverb:
"A merry heart doeth good like a medicine: but a broken
spirit drieth the bones" (Prov. 17:22).

> Last year was, to coin a phrase, "the best of years and at
> the same time, the worst of years" for me. It was the most
> stressful period of my life. I graduated from college in
> December, and was going to the seminary while I waited
> for my fiancée to graduate (we were planing to get married
> in August). But as if that weren't enough, while home on
> spring break, I had a ganglion on my wrist. It was just a
> little growth and didn't concern me much. At that time I
> was more concerned about my dad who had just discov-
> ered cancer of the prostrate.
>
> After break, I went back to school, where, two weeks later
> I got a call from the doctor telling me I had broken all the
> odds, and the growth he thought harmless was a rare form
> of melanoma, and I would need two operations and exten-
> sive cobalt treatments.
>
> Talk about stress! I had barely hung up the telephone
> when Mother called and informed me that Dad's cancer
> was extensive, and he would have only two or three years
> to live.

The quotation is from a paper written by one of my

students dealing with life's haunting, stressful, pivotal experiences. However, the fascinating thing about that paper was the strategy the young man devised to deal with his troubles.

> You know the worst thing about it was that I could not bring myself to cry. Instead I found myself laughing. Does it seem sacrilegious or senseless to you? For me, laughter became a way of dealing with stress. It was the best way I knew to accept my humanity, and take life seriously. The stress isn't so bad now. I survived the operations and cobalt, and doctors have modified their diagnosis on Dad. I'm married and am not even working as hard. Laughter, I believe, is God's tool given to help us not only to minister but to survive.
>
> There's a little prayer I found, which I repeat often:
>
> Love God.
> Ponder Scripture.
> Meditate on Christ.
> Follow the Spirit.
> Encourage others.
> Cherish yourself.
> Enjoy life.
> Mediate Christian compassion.
> And, when appropriate,
> Don't forget to dance![1]

Neither my positive, pleasant friend (referred to earlier) nor my student, who found in laughter a means for survival, believe in magic nor see in a sense of humor a panacea for all life's troubles. To contend that you can "grin and bear it," or "laugh your troubles away," may be a form of cruelty in which the healthy can indulge, but shows neither compassion nor honesty. Life is complex and often puzzling, and is tough enough without having to endure such counsel. Maybe you're trying to adjust to the devastating reality of an impending divorce, a diagnosis of a malignancy, or a drug problem with a child. You need love and compassion, not cheap advice. You've already had to deal with anger, despair, rebellion, and tears. Don't let those natural emotions create guilt within you. All of us experience these emotions during such times of stress. Don't despair; life will improve. You're not alone in your struggle. A God of love is on your side.

Still, there is the medicine of a "merry heart," and it can do you good. There are four principles connected with this remedy, and they merit careful consideration.

First, while the medicine of a merry heart will not cure all your maladies, it can make them easier to bear. Abraham Lincoln, one of our more sensitive and compassionate presidents, upon being criticized during the darkest days of the Civil War for his stories, jokes, and light touch, replied, "I laugh because I cannot cry." Lincoln's ability to survive and serve effectively, despite his depressive tendencies, is in itself remarkable.

My most poignant experiences in ministry have had to do with young men in the military, assigned to battlefront duty, laughing, teasing, and bantering each other to keep from crying. Their mirth was a studied way of keeping back their tears. I shall never forget a night at Travis Air Force Base when scores of young servicemen were leaving for Vietnam. I remember their heroism and courage as well as their clever wit and hilarious horseplay. As a candid friend of mine used to say, "There are times when a sense of humor can keep you from going mad."

Second, there are times when the medicine of a "merry

heart" can facilitate health, but always it blesses those who love us and those with whom we work. I have a friend dying of cancer. I visit him and try to help, but he's the one helping me. Even when I try to thank him, he has a way of fending me off. His sense of humor gives me courage, and makes me want to reach out and try to love every needy person I meet. But you say, his sense of humor isn't healing him, and you are both right and wrong. You're right in that his laughter hasn't stopped the spread of the deadly malignancy that is destroying his body, but you're wrong in failing to note the healing of life his purposeful joy is bringing to me and all who know him, let alone what it does for his inner spirit. Is his humor and joy part of the light "that shineth more and more unto the perfect day"? (Prov. 4:18).

There are, however, instances, and indeed many of them, where laughter has brought healing of the body, as well as the spirit. Some years ago, Dr. Raymond A. Moody wrote a best-seller, *Life After Life,* in which he argued that modern medicine has concentrated too heavily on such things as aches and pains, drugs and surgery, techniques and technology, and not enough on hope, trust, understanding, love, and joy. Dr. Moody's story of the famous clown who frequently visits children's hospitals is revealing and haunting. A small girl, who had spoken to no one for months, was being fed by a nurse one evening when the clown walked into her room. The child recognized the clown at once, became so fascinated with his conversation and antics that suddenly she began talking. That was the key that led to her recovery. Every clown can tell you stories of people brought back from extreme states of withdrawal by laughter.

You may be aware of Norman Cousins's (the former editor of *Saturday Review*) experiences. Back in 1964, he became ill of what is called "Collagen Illness," a disease of the connective tissues. He suffered great pain, and his condition was getting worse. After extensive treatment and no improvement, he finally decided the hospital was no place for him. He checked himself out and changed his medication to megadoses of vitamin C, laughter, humor, and fun. His nurse would show him old "Candid Camera" films, read him stories from E. B. and Katherine White's *Subtreasury of American Humor,* and otherwise endeavor to make him joyful. Cousins made the discovery that ten minutes of deep laughter had an anesthetic effect and would give him at least two hours of pain-free sleep. When the effect wore off, the nurse would show the films again. Cousins came to see the healing power of laughter, emotional well-being, positive attitudes, joy, hope, peace, and contentment. Perhaps you have read of his experiences in *Anatomy of an Illness* and *The Healing Heart.*

While the medical community was skeptical at first, today there are many hospitals where "laughter therapy" is being used with positive results. Cousins now often lectures at medical schools.

"At DeKalb General Hospital in Decatur, Georgia, patients who seem close to giving up are getting an unusual prescription these days: a few hours in the humor room." The above sentence marks the opening of an intriguing article in the June, 1987, issue of the AARP News Bulletin.[2] The "humor room" is described as a cheerful, brightly lit room where videotapes of old movies, reruns of "Candid Camera," and videocassettes of comedians Red Skelton, Abbott and Costello, and Bob Hope are shown. Sometimes patients who had no desire to get well, after spending a few days in "the humor room," suddenly said, "I want to get well and go home." "Hospitals are beginning to discover the positive power of humor," observed educator Joel Goodman.[3]

Interestingly, the therapeutic power of humor is not really a recent discovery; we're just beginning to verify in the laboratory what perceptive people have always sensed. Do you remember the old man in *Tom Sawyer* who "laughed loud and joyously, shook up the details of his anatomy from head to foot," and argued that such laughter was "money in a man's pocket" at least in the sense of cutting down on the doctors' bills. Perhaps Mark Twain was more of a psychiatrist than he knew.

Humor helps in many ways: making people feel good about themselves, relieving stress, and contributing to relaxation. Laughter not only brings emotional and mental benefits, there are physiological benefits as well: easing of muscular tension, stimulating the respiratory system, and increasing oxygen in the blood. Laughter has been shown to lower blood pressure. Laughter is "good exercise." Perhaps future research will demonstrate many other ways laughter can help bodily healing. As the village wit put it, "Laugh all you can. It will extend your life; there is no record of anyone who has died laughing."

Third, a merry heart is more fun for us and for others. All of us know this but how rarely do we practice it? Is your life as joyful as it might be? If not, why not? Is it our Puritan heritage which too often assumes pleasure is synonymous with evil. "If it's fun, it's either sinful, fattening, or expensive." I wonder how many times I have heard that across the years. Does responding gloomily, defeatedly, or

sadly take less effort? Perhaps it has to do with our childhood. Some learn it early and easily; others struggle to live
by it all their years. "We learned at home to laugh and
play as well as to work and cry," observes a friend of mine.
"My parents valued the merry heart, the soft touch, even
the mischievous grin. When someone affronted us, we
made a joke of it, and soon forgot it. My Dad used to say,
'Don't let monkeys make a monkey out of you. That's my
philosophy!' Then he'd grin and say, 'I always feel like
apologizing to the monkeys when I make a statement like
that.' "

What kind of people do you like to be with? What are
the qualities that mark the best leader you know? Who
among your friends is the one you enjoy the most? You
know: the confident, joyful, happy, and relaxed individual.
My strongest reinforcement in pursuing the life of joy is
in arranging to be with joyful people. There are people
we'd walk across town to visit, and others we'd walk three
blocks to miss. I've had so many wonderful friends. Take
"George," for example. His nickname was "Jelly." You'd
think with a name like that he'd be ruined, but not George.
He was a magnificent after-dinner speaker, a professional
master of ceremonies. He was "on the circuit" and could
command handsome honorariums, yet he spent a great
deal of his time working "for free" for civic and church
groups: Boy Scouts, Little League, service clubs, church
dinners. To listen to him you'd think he was being paid a
thousand dollars for each appearance. It was his way of
saying *thank you* to God and to life. He never used his
humor in a deprecating or degrading way. He did not
belittle or embarrass. Humor was his gift, and he took
great joy in sharing it.

George had a talk entitled "The Sixth Sense," which I often heard him give. The more I heard it, the better I liked it. "Everybody is aware of the five senses," he'd say. "But there are others like 'horse sense' and 'common sense,' but tonight I'm speaking on another: 'a sense of humor.' " I could almost give George's talk. He had what he called "the fallout from a sense of humor." He'd say:

Humor lightens the load, and adds spice to life.
Humor gives perspective in a crisis and takes the sting out of things that hurt.
Humor helps your wife tolerate you when you're not very lovely.
Humor improves theology and makes religion easier to bear.
Humor makes the kitchen cooler and your in-laws nicer.
Humor will even improve your looks when you glance in the mirror.

Finally, remember: Jesus had a merry heart, and He wants us to have one, too. He said, "These things have I spoken unto you, that my joy might remain in you, and that your joy might be full" (John 15:11). Why do so many people make religion so dreary? My Bible says that after God created the earth and mankind, He said to Himself, *It is good, very good.* Everything about the gospel has to do with joy. And the Bible says, "The joy of the Lord is your strength" (Neh. 8:10).

Samuel Johnson was right, "The size of a man's understanding may always be justly measured by his mirth." Since no man is a hypocrite in his pleasures, his laughter tells us what kind of person he is.

Would you like to do more than *"make* it through the day"? Say, *"win* it through the day"?

A Prescription for You

1. *Learn to laugh as well as pray.*
2. *Share your pleasures.*
3. *Be generous with your love if you can, but at least smile.*
4. *Make your praise joyful.*

4   The Two Sides of Loneliness
Loneliness

"The only abnormality is the incapacity to love."
—Anais Nin

The place is Truman Plaza, and it's located on the corner of Clay Allee and Hutton Weg across the street from Clay Command Headquarters and near the great Grunewald Forrest. Truman Plaza is an unusual place, a shopping center for six thousand American troops and their families who are stationed in West Berlin. My wonderful German friend, who says the American, French, and British soldiers make West Berlin the safest city in the world, calls it "Little America." But the first Saturday we took bus 11 and visited Truman Plaza, we felt for many it was one of the loneliest places in the world. West Berlin is a beautiful, peaceable, orderly, safe city but surrounded by a ninety-nine-mile concrete wall and East German troops, and located right in the middle of Communist East Germany. Stop, sit down, and speak in a clear US accent, and someone will stop, and ask you where you're from, when have you been there, and wait with eager eyes and ears for your answer. He doesn't want you to speak German; it's the colloquial English he longs to hear. It's a

lonely place but a friendly place where people reach out
to each other.

Lonely, lonely people! They're everywhere. They're old
and young and everywhere in between. Who is the loneliest? The university student, those who are divorced, the
single mother, the elderly? I'm not certain, but my vote
would go with the young and the old. There's the haunting
horror of teenage suicide and the depression of the segre-
gated old folks. Walk down the hallway of any nursing
home and count the number of people who try to speak
to you, or pick out a sad-eyed child and engage her in
conversation.

I grew up in a small town where everyone thought they
knew me, but no one knew me at all. During high school,
I worked weekends in a coffee shop. While serving up the
pecan pie, I would tell my customers that one day I would
move to France. I dreamed of escape. My white uniform,
black nylon apron with grease stains, white rubber-soled
shoes—they were my prison uniform. The town, I
thought, was my prison cell. My way of coping with the
present was to ignore it. By the time I went to college, I
was unable to relate to the people around me. I circled
inward in ever tighter knots, took in nothing that might
infringe on my private world.

Then I married a man I'd known since I was sixteen.
I married because I was under the illusion that a husband
would end my loneliness. Some people have children for
the same reason, and it is painful to learn that children,
husbands, or wives are only a distraction from loneliness
and not a cure. I imagined, as John Fowles says of the
Victorian lovers in *French Lieutenant's Woman,* that my
husband and I would lie for days in each other's arms in
some jasmine-scented room, "infinitely alone, exiled, yet

fused in that loneliness, inseparable in that exile." I married him not for what he was, but for what I wanted to become with him. I should have known better. But even after all these years, I still think, from time to time, that some man can save me.

I wanted to know how to love realistically, but I had no idea of where to begin. We need love, we need affection, and it is because of the misconceptions and fantasies we have about love, because of the distorted search and the broken dreams, that we sometimes cry out in our sleep.

When the marriage ended, I had to face a new and worse kind of loneliness. It pounced on me with all its might and simply would not let go.[1]

What is loneliness? Loneliness is when you are forced to be alone against your will: solitude is when you are willingly alone.

William Sadler, Jr., has divided loneliness into categories: *interpersonal*—when you miss someone you love; *social*—when you're excluded from a group; *cultural* —when you feel cut off from a tradition; *cosmic*—when you feel the universe is absurd, life is pointless, and God is lost; *psychological*—when you feel alienated from yourself and out of touch with your true nature. Sadler says,

> In each case, the person perceived himself to be cut off from another person, from himself, a group, a tradition, a universe, a god. So when the person says, "I feel lonely," well, you have to ask: "Where do you feel lonely?"[2]

All of us know the difference between loneliness and aloneness. We feel comfortable when we are simply alone. We choose to be alone. But loneliness is something else entirely. It's when we are alone and don't choose to be. It's when we want to be included and feel left out. It's when we long to belong and somehow feel we don't.

All of us recognize the necessity of aloneness if we are to be balanced, healthy, productive human beings. There must be a necessary aloneness at the center of our being. We each must find our own identity, come to terms with ourselves, acknowledge our value and worth, accept our humanity, and face the fact that we are accountable and responsible. I must claim my own unique personhood if I am to recognize the personhood in others. I must first examine my own soul in silence if I am to reach out to others in understanding and love. I am responsible for myself, and until I come to terms with that, I cannot claim my place in the community. Otherwise, I will forever be alienating you precisely because I see you in terms of my own psychosis.

There are many things that aggravate loneliness in our culture. Take our mobility. One in five Americans changes homes annually and nearly half do every five years. In 1960, the average professional held three jobs in his career; today, the figure has risen to 4.2 jobs and continues to rise. The other day I read about a girl who lived in forty-two states before the seventh grade and how she learned "quick-entry techniques" and the pain of making too-deep friendships.

A sense of community is what we find among the people who know us, with whom we feel safe. That rarely includes the neighbors, but this was not always so. For most of history, human beings found their sense of community where they lived, with the people among whom they were born and with whom they died. But most of us who live in the city and suburb live one place, and find "community" in another. Or nowhere.

For many decades, European observers have been struck by the gregariousness of Americans. As they would travel across America they would notice particularly the family's propensity for "sitting on the front porch," in contrast to the Europeans' walled gardens and love of privacy. Americans seem to them to have no objection to being publicly displayed, indeed they seem to enjoy it. They have nothing of which they are ashamed, and if other people can see them, they can see others in return. The instinct seemed to gratify their instinct for sociability. Yet, ironically, for many reasons, this custom has largely disappeared. First, the porch was screened in, then glassed in, and finally curtained so the draperies could be pulled. Indeed, the porch became another room, and where funds were sufficient, walls were built.

There are many external forces that contribute to our loneliness—the pervasive secularism of our culture, our obsession with individual rights, identity, and doing our own thing, mobility, our dependence upon externals to bring us satisfaction, the stresses in our competitive life-styles, and so forth. Yet there have always been outside factors that have had to be confronted and dealt with. And we must also deal realistically with the fact that all of us must discover ourselves in our aloneness. All of life's ultimate decisions must be made in solitariness. We are not permitted the luxury of turning them over to someone else. When we try we only cripple ourselves and add to the other person's misery.

People who try to be something to everybody end up being nothing to anybody. We must come to terms with ourselves, know who we are, and find meaning and purpose in living, achieving, and serving. How did Marcus Aurelius put it? "Weak men seek retreats; strong men carry them with them."

There are scores of illustrations of this truth. Take, for example, Debussy and Cezanne. Debussy developed his own special creativity in disciplined aloneness. He never visited Spain, yet his friend and interpreter George Copeland affirmed, "His *Iberia* is more Spanish than any Spanish music that has ever been written by her countrymen."

The life of Cezanne, with his enforced isolation, seems so hard and barren. Until he was fifty, Cezanne's paintings, on which he labored for months, were given in exchange for groceries. An art supplier accepted some in trade for tubes of paint. Today every first-rate museum in the world prizes Cezanne's works as eternal treasures. He was a bold innovator, a courageous pioneer who withdrew and refused to surrender the image God had put in his heart and mind.

Let us neither spurn nor despise our aloneness. Here we may find our truest being.

The first step in conquering loneliness lies in confronting the problem realistically.

Honesty about one's emotions is rarely easy, and sometimes the primary cause of my loneliness is outside me rather than inside me. Yet nearly always it has more to do with my own sense of inadequacy than with something someone else has done, intentionally or unintentionally. Projecting the cause upon someone or something else can be a way of saving face, but at the same time, it may be a way of avoiding the issue and leaving the problem untouched.

Part of our problem with loneliness lies in our desiring things that are mutually exclusive. For example, most of us want mobility, privacy, and convenience. However, these are things that actually mitigate against community. Sociologist Phillip Slater says, "The car did more than anything else to destroy community life in America." How can you move all the time and build relationships with other people?

The problem of the automobile and its depersonalizing effects upon human personality is illustrated in an experience Walter Cronkite had. Cronkite tells of being viciously sideswiped one afternoon by a blue-and-white four-door sedan with a dent in the right front door. At a dinner party that night, hosted by a biology professor of impeccable courtesy, Cronkite recounted the incident. All present agreed that even civilized men often can become brutes when protected and hidden by two tons of steel. As the evening ended, the host offered his guest a ride home—in his blue-and-white four-door sedan which, Cronkite noticed as he got in, had a dent in the right front door.[3]

Or take our desire for convenience. Terri Schultz tells of the locksmith who arrived to put a deadbolt lock on the front door of her apartment in New York City. As he got out his drill and bits to go to work, he asked her if she lived alone. When she replied that she did, he began to talk about the New Yorkers he meets who live alone with multiple locks on their doors and iron bars on their windows. There are seven-hundred thousand of them in New York City and most of them live in fear. Finally the man turned to Terri Schultz and asked, "Why do you live alone?" and she replied, "Because I am more free, more independent." He responded, "You don't have freedom, all you have is convenience."[4]

We might as well be realistic with ourselves. We must decide what we want and then learn to live with the consequences of our choices. To have community we must limit our mobility, restrict our privacy, and interfere with our convenience.

Any cure for loneliness must begin inside me.

I think the thing that brought this home to me was discovering early in my ministry that the loneliest, most depressed people are not always the people who had most reason to feel lonely. Often they seemed far more favorable situated than others who appeared less plagued by loneliness. Loneliness has to do more with inner feelings than with outward circumstances. Despite the fact that most of us begin with the idea that our loneliness comes from causes outside ourselves: how others treat us, how they feel about us, or respond to us—such is not really the case.

It is only reasonable to expect that some will respond to us with understanding and generosity, and others will respond to us with indifference and even hostility. Indeed, that's the way we respond to others. The only thing constant about each of us is our inner consciousness. Our age, size, looks, and health—these change with the years; only our consciousness remains constant. It's what happens within that consciousness that makes the difference. This is the reason that any cure for loneliness must begin within us.

The sooner we stop blaming others: husbands, wives, parents, children, and bosses; the sooner we will begin to master our loneliness. I like the teenager's comment: "I was thinking of all these horrible things about my parents when suddenly it hit me—if they're all that bad, how come I'm so wonderful?"

People who live fully will accept their pain and learn to live with it and use it as best they can. Abraham Lincoln and Dag Hammarskjöld suffered from periodic, massive depression, and Winston Churchill once referred to depression as his "lap dog." Alienation is within before it is without, and the cure must begin within.

I need to be honest about my need for and my fear of community.

Boys who consider themselves homely or ordinary looking normally will not approach a girl whom they consider beautiful for fear of being rejected. They only approach girls whom they consider in their league. However, psychologists tell us that the beautiful girl often feels unattractive, and if approached would respond just as readily as the homely girl.

Community requires effort, courage, initiative, and a willingness to reach out, become involved, and take risks. All human relationships involve vulnerability. Many refrain from marriage, parenthood, and friendship precisely for these reasons.

The way to conquer a fear is to confront it and do something about it.

Overcoming the barriers that divide is a lifetime task.

We'll be working at it as long as we live. Conquer prejudice in one area and it pops up in another. It is part of the human equation. We are island bound and require God's grace to see into the other person's heart.

To understand your wife, husband, child, or friend is a task requiring forever. Bridging the chasm that divides is a permanent part of humanity and community.

Seeking community in the abstract is always doomed to failure. Community is people and I find community only when I find other people. Community begins with God's love for me and my love for all His children.

The ultimate belonging is to God. How can we love others unless we are certain He loves us? The community that overcomes loneliness begins ultimately in God's love for me and my love for all His other children. This is the final belonging, and without it I shall always be homeless in this universe. But this truth can be hard to grasp and more difficult to practice.

Telling people God loves them isn't enough either to cure loneliness or to liberate people for more productive and joyful living. Now don't misunderstand me, it is the goodness of God that leads to repentance, and His love that makes forgiveness possible and triggers healing in the human heart. But that love can only be apprehended and claimed when grounded and made tangible through other human beings. God is our friend, but the reality of that truth can only be understood by way of the friendship of other human beings.

Velma Darbo Stevens in her book: *A Fresh Look at Loneliness,*[5] told of a young, blonde Norwegian friend who—like her father—felt called to the ministry, gave up his job, and entered the seminary. She, as a young girl with her parents in the seminary, remembered the young man always singing, "No longer lonely! No longer lonely! For Jesus is the friend of friends to me." Yet, she pointed out, he was the loneliest person she knew, and he soon dropped out of the seminary. Looking back, Mrs. Stevens observed, Jesus was the Norwegian's friend, yet ironically he never learned how to make earthly friends, even among other

Christians. Was he conditioned from childhood to despise himself or trained not to trust other people, or was there so much hostility within him he could not relate lovingly to other people? We cannot say but we do know that it isn't enough to tell a lonely person Jesus is his friend. God's love must be embodied in other people if it is to be comprehended. The heart of the gospel is the incarnation: God assuming our flesh, and the community of faith is called "the body of Christ." We are His hands, His feet, and His heart for lonely human beings.

Treasure your aloneness. Make solitude your friend. That's one side, but there's another side: face your loneliness and work for the community you need. Be a friend and be friendly.

Something You Can Do About Loneliness

1. *Even when life is unfair, reject self-pity.*
2. *Refuse to allow loneliness to dominate your life.*
3. *To have friends, you must be friendly.*
4. *Get involved with other people.*
5. *Move from "I need somebody to care for me" to "I want to care for somebody."*

5 I'm Feeling Mighty Low!
Depression

"I'm telling myself a sad story about myself."
—An eight-year-old

There's nothing funny about depression, least of all a depressed child whose sad eyes and sagging lips reveal a lonely hurt. Childhood meant for discovery, excitement, joy has become anguish and pain.

You must experience depression to comprehend the anguish it can bring. Those who ridicule or deprecate it have not experienced it. Called by many names: "the black dog," "the blue mood," "the life of gloom;" depression steals upon us, like a London "pea-souper," a fog that engulfs us, suffocates us, and fills us with gloom. Life loses all its joy and often we wish to die. (Sixty percent of all suicides are depressed.)

Clinical depression, sometimes called "the common cold of emotional illness," affects all ages and all socioeconomic classes. Thirty to forty million Americans, twice as many women as men, will experience it at least once in life. Approximately two percent of all children and six to seven percent of all adolescents will be plagued by it. Depression has been termed "the twentieth century plague."

No respecter of persons both in antiquity and modern times, depression victims seem endless: King Saul, Elijah, Job, Jeremiah, Abraham Lincoln, Winston Churchill, and Ernest Hemingway, to name a few. Brilliance, creativity, affluence—none of these can ward it off. They may actually increase vulnerability. If you've never experienced it, be thankful and glad. At some time in life, the odds are that either you or someone you love will struggle with this black emotion.

Many have called him "the lionhearted," but Winston Churchill did not see himself as such. "It was the nation and the race dwelling all around the globe that had the lion's heart; I had the luck to be called upon to give the roar."[1]

Churchill adored his parents but was neglected by both of them. While still a child he was sent away to a brutal boarding school in Ascot where the headmaster caned him until his back was a mass of welts. He was abused by other boys. Toward the end of his life, in halting tones, he told his doctor about it. Sickly and poorly coordinated, speaking with a lisp and slight stutter, he was at the mercy of bullies. They beat him, ridiculed him, and pelted him with cricket balls. Trembling and humiliated he hid in a nearby woods. At times he despaired. He suffered from chest ailments and boils. For most of his life he had to sleep nude between silk sheets or his body would break out in welts. Yet he had a great memory, a love of the English language, and a rare sense of humor. Sometimes he chose the rapier approach. At a dinner party Lady Astor once said to him, "Winston, if I were your wife I'd poison your soup." He replied, "Nancy, if I were your husband I'd drink it." He spoke of "dull, duller, Dulles." He called

Attlee, "a sheep in sheep's clothing." He spent endless hours preparing his speeches. He lost more elections than any other politician of his time and twice switched parties. Yet in time of national disaster, perhaps more than any other man, he saved his nation.

All Churchill's life he was plagued by depression. At the most inappropriate times he would sink into black moods like Lincoln, Goethe, Tolstoy, Robert E. Lee, and Martin Luther. To him it was "the black dog" that chased at his heels and wrought havoc in his life. Yet this man spoke the words and embodied the courage that gave a nation a new lease on life and hope.

Are you sympathetic with Winston Churchill? Has his "black dog" of depression ever run at your heels? It is timeless and universal. Sooner or later all mortals have to confront it, either in themselves or in someone they love. Living with it can make death seem preferable.

How do we respond when we are confronted with this dark emotion? For example, if I were to confess I had been depressed, how would you feel about the matter? Indifferent? Critical? Casual? Sympathetic? Obsessed? Would you think, *If he had been smarter, wiser, or more astute he would have never got himself into such a situation?* You might well be correct, but would offer little help, for I know that too. Or would you think, *Oh, God, then maybe he can help me!* At least you would know where I have been and be open to what I might tell you. Most responses center around one of two polarities: either we are desperate, or we couldn't care less.

Sooner or later few will escape. Nearly everybody, at some time, becomes plagued by the dark emotion, sometimes to the point of desperation, and I can assure you if you never experience it, some member of your family will. Depression is epidemic among teenagers and young adults. At this moment we are experiencing a wave of adolescent suicides, and nearly all older people experience some depression. (Carl Menninger points out that every year more people commit suicide than are murdered.) Some have contended that depression is more prevalent among the highly intelligent and creative than other groups, and it is certainly true that high achievers, the conscientious (those who set high standards for themselves), seem to be "sitting ducks" for the black mood. So many of the great men of the Bible, at critical moments in their lives, were depressed. Moses asked God to take his life, Job despaired, Elijah wanted to die, John the Baptist lost his courage, and I guess you would call Jeremiah, the great Old Testament prophet, "the most miserable one of all." Each of them can be a study in how to handle this devastating reality.

Depression has been called the vocational hazard of the helping professions. In many ways, it is "the dominant mood of the age." One theological professor says that it is a problem for 70 percent of the young ministers in his seminary classes. Abusing the body takes an inevitable toll on the emotions. "Depression is tied to our physiology as much as our psychology," he says. For the pastor, Monday morning is often marked by the "postadrenalin blues." Then there is the inherent loneliness of any leadership position. There is self-recrimination and biochemical imbalance. The professor contends that depression can have helpful and healthy results if it slows us down, forces us to confront destructive patterns of behavior, and demonstrates to us the necessity for diversion and recreation.

There are varied degrees of depression and differing kinds. *Endogenous* (internally generated) *depression* which is biochemical, and often inherited, at least in the sense that there seems to be a combination of elements that make it likely, results when the brain and nervous system become disorganized. Increasingly, we are discovering defects in body chemistry, specifically in the neurotransmitters that link nerve to nerve, which appear to cause depression. There is *reactive depression* which results from a real or symbolic loss. It is basically a mourning or grief situation. It may come from loss of a job or a threat to one's professional standing, retirement, a divorce, a geographic uprooting, or the death of a loved one. Then there is *neurotic depression* which results from exhaustion of adaptation, severe or prolonged stress, unresolved conflict, or chronic anxiety. Many doctors now believe that victims of depression carry an innate susceptibility to the disease. The disease can be triggered by external factors or by changes in the body's own chemistry. Manic depression, for example, can be a family legacy.

Many things can trigger depression, some real and some imagined. Depression can stem from guilt over things which are not our fault, rejection, loneliness, losing a job, or financial adversity. However, it is the person's reaction to the events—not the events—which causes depression, and depression is always a lack of self-esteem. The feeling of being worthwhile is a human being's most precious possession. Symptoms of depression include a hopeless feeling on arising, loss of interest in a vocational or avocational activity, a hopeless feeling about the future, self-pity and self-criticism, irritability, indecisiveness, procrastination, insomnia or its opposite, loss of appetite and loss of interest in life, and loss of desire to live.

Nearly always these reactions are involved in depression: (1) *Self-blame.* The depressed person is inclined to blame himself and not others for his troubles. Indeed, he might come nearer to finding help if he could turn upon someone else and vent his hurt and hostility. (2) *Inability to make decisions.* A really depressed person simply cannot decide, and if he does he spends endless hours worrying about what he has done. (3) *Depression is basically anger turned inward.* The person has lost something very valuable, feels he has, and is angry with himself for his stupidity or fault. He turns in upon himself. (4) *Helplessness.* This feeling seems to be nurtured by the depressed person and most psychiatrists believe the patient must get involved with purposeful activities if he is to make progress. (5) *Mourning and grief because of a sense of loss.*

It will help us to bear in mind that there are different levels of depression. In mild depression, we can continue to function normally; we can tolerate the feeling. Medium depression begins to affect us. We start canceling out on our obligations. In severe depression, people are totally incapacitated and unable to take care of themselves. They won't eat. They refuse contact with other people. And the wish to die is so strong that suicide is a real threat.

When you realize you are depressed, what action should you take? The first step is to recognize your depression. You will need the help of someone who loves you. Since depression is a signal that you have lost something, the sooner you become aware of what it is and how to do something about it the better off you will be. The second step is to face and accept the reality of the loss. Third, develop a perspective on the loss. Finally, it is likely you will have to have help, both medical and psychological, and the sooner you get it the better.

Depression does not mean merely "feeling blue or down." Every person has low moments and difficult times. Clinical depression is a form of emotional illness with relatively clear symptoms: a devastating loss of self-confidence and self-esteem, a deep sense of personal failure, and a feeling of despair so severe that it is nearly paralyzing or causes suicidal tendencies.

Students of human nature have long pointed out that one of the major causes is the loss of a love object, but clinical experience has shown many other causes such as the breakup of a love affair, some professional or financial setback, some social humiliation, and the loss of a loved one or a job. How can such dissimilar events cause the same illness? Soren Kierkegaard, the gloomy Dane, pointed out long ago that we suffer not so much over the loss of the person as over the depletion of ourselves. How can we live without that which we have lost? Our whole being is threatened. Depression has been defined as "complete absorption with oneself," going even deeper and deeper into one's own misery.

With some reluctance, I confess I have been there. I know now that I contributed to the journey. At times it can be easier to choose hopelessness, the humiliation of frustration, failure, and even defeat. I turned my disappointment and anger in upon myself, and before I knew it, I was doing deadly things to myself and those I love. A strange and unrecognized obsession with oneself, brings only pain to those who love us. "Doing what comes naturally" can be the deadliest of all choices in depression. What you want to do is withdraw, cease to function as far as you can, live in your misery and gloom, and in a very real sense, die. But this only aggravates the problem. You must force yourself to stay active, keep yourself involved with others, carefully follow a routine, take vigorous physical exercise, and find someone you trust who will keep reminding you that depression is cyclic; it too will pass, the old joys will return, and life will be challenging and sweet again. If you have someone who will be loyal, honest and loving, patient and firm, insisting on your routine and conquering strategy, then you are fortunate indeed.

There are encouraging facts about depression to remember:

- *Depression can be treated.* Indeed there are many new and improved ways of dealing with it. Find a good physician and take his or her counsel.
- *Depression is nearly always cyclic.* It, too, will pass. The old pleasures will return. Cherish this fact in your darkest hours.
- *Depression is rarely fatal; we just wish we could die.* Depression magnifies your miseries and convinces you that you are more desperate than you really are.
- *Depression is hell for those we love.* Work at helping them find as much encouragement and pleasure as possible. Try not to pile all your gloom upon them.
- *Accept the fact that depression triggers self-centered behavior and magnifies one's preoccupation with oneself.*

You see, without being aware of it, my perfectionism

had enticed me into choosing gloom rather than accepting lowered standards of work. It was as if I were saying, "Since I can't do it perfectly, I won't do it at all." Had I seen this in the beginning, I would of course have avoided depression.

Perhaps my standard had been higher because I felt I was doing God's work. However, healing did not come until I accepted the fact that my goals might not be God's, and if I had made a vocational choice where I could not achieve my goals, I had to live with that fact.

As strange as it may seem, I who had given my life to the service of God, a God of limitless love, had little love for myself. In a sense I was refusing to accept my humanity, to trust and not be afraid, to reward myself as well as blame myself. When I moved into a real world—which incidentally is the world of God's grace—healing came.

Depression is almost always treatable, yet only one person in five seek help. How can this be altered? How can we recognize it in ourselves and others? The symptoms are marked: feelings of hopelessness and helplessness, loss of interest in life, inability to concentrate, change in eating and sleeping habits, chronic pain without apparent cause, anger at oneself, and thoughts of suicide and death. If such feelings persist then we need help. We can help our children learn to like themselves, talk to us about their feelings and needs, and share with us their anxieties. The cure for depression includes proper medication, love of others, and learning to love ourselves.

Believe me there is sunlight at the end of the tunnel! I know, I've been there. Almost daily, medical progress is being made in this field. Elijah left his juniper bush, and in time, you will too. Then you will be "a wounded healer" opening the door for others to find healing and health.

Conquering the Dark Emotion

1. *Stop punishing yourself; that only makes matters worse.*
2. *Confront your emotions. If you've lost something, if you're angry, if you feel guilty, find out why and act.*
3. *Keep a routine.*
4. *Don't withdraw. Get real exercise and diversion.*
5. *Accept God's grace, and enjoy it.*

6   Barefoot on a Hot Tin Roof
Stress

"Adaptability is probably the most distinctive characteristic of life."

—Hans Selye

We live in a pressure-cooker world. Stress seems our way of life. Most of us feel it every day when our kids are late leaving for school, when we get caught in traffic with a deadline hanging over us, when our boss chews us out, when we discover we're overdrafted at the bank, and when our safety, security, or comfort are threatened. To face a challenge, to confront a problem, to acknowledge the risks of being alive—all of these can create stress. However, life completely without stress would be death. (Nothing is so relaxed as a corpse.) Our goal is not to eliminate stress but to live with it healthily, productively, and indeed, to make it our friend. Hans Selye, the Viennese physician who did such monumental work on stress at McGill University, Montreal, contended stress can be "the spice of life."[1]

Yet ironically, stress can contribute to some devastating human problems such as illness, emotional instability, and depression. Stress can be linked to arthritis, ulcers, kidney, heart and circulatory problems, migraine headaches, and other illnesses. The real cause is not stress but our reaction to it, when stress becomes what Selye termed "dis-stress." Selye, who studied in Prague, Paris, and Rome, came in 1932 to McGill where he discovered the first evidence of his stress theory. His great work was done while serving as professor and director of the Institute of Experimental Medicine and Surgery at McGill. He was a buoyant, exciting human being. Almost to the end, he'd arise at 4:00 AM every morning and bicycle around the campus, despite his bout with cancer and two artificial hips. He came to believe adaptability is one of our greatest assets and powers, a secret of happy and useful living.

Despite the impression left in contemporary self-help books, stress is not a modern phenomenon. While cave people did not have traffic congestion, the atomic bomb, the stock market, and taxes to worry about, they had violence, insecurity, disease, hunger, and many other frightening things we seldom think about. Perhaps they had more stress, not less. We are conscious of ours, and that may increase its potential for doing us harm.

Again, it is not the amount of stress that causes our problem but how we respond to it. Stress diseases are diseases of adaptation because they are due not to any particular stressor but to our faulty adaptive response. Stress is the nonspecific demand of the body to any demand made upon it. The "nonspecific demand" is the essence of the problem. We can't avoid stress, but we can learn to react in a healthy manner, see it as an opportunity and a challenge, and even sometimes a joy.

Perhaps the place to begin is with your own stress chart. What causes you anxiety, fills you with apprehension, causes tightness in the pit of your stomach? What makes you want to scream, jump out the window, hit something or somebody? While many good stress charts are available, each of us needs to work out our own assigning to each item a stress quotient. Take the following list, place the items in order of significance, and rate them from 1 to 100. Examine your feelings and add to the list other items that cause you trouble.

- Death
- Divorce
- Loss of job
- Debilitating injury
- Professional or business failure
- Caring for an abnormal child
- Guilt
- Threat to Life
- Unrealistic Expectations
- Loss of Social Status
- Loss of Meaningful Relationships

No one can make an adequate stress list for someone else for many varied factors such as backgrounds, circumstances, inner needs, and personal feelings vary from person to person. What disturbs you may not disturb me, but both your feelings and mine are important.

When I say it is not stress as such that does the damage but our response to it, I am in no way minimizing the pain or implying there are easy solutions. There are no pat and easy answers. Take, for example, the young executive who is bypassed in promotion and senses immediately a decline in status in the company hierarchy and disappointment at home, especially if he grew up in a family where love and approval were parceled out on an achievement basis.

What if no one in his home or circle of friends senses his loss of self-esteem? There have been times, in extreme cases, where such a scenario led to suicide.

Perhaps an even more prevalent example might be the highly educated mother who gives up a career to rear children, but she finds the demands, tedium, and grubby work almost more than she can endure. Add to that an insensitive husband who makes unreasonable demands upon her. Or, what about the fifty-five-year-old who gets the pink slip with children still in college and goes for months or even years without work? Such pressures can be devastating.

In times of stress, have you ever tried relating to Bible characters? How do you think Eve felt when Adam blamed her for eating the forbidden fruit? (Some contend men are still blaming women for all their problems.) Consider Elijah, the bold man of God. When confronted by the prophets of Baal he was as fearless as lion, but when defied by Queen Jezebel he ran like a rabbit. There are a variety of external and internal forces which affect our responses in stressful times. David appeared to have lived most of his life under stress. Was this part of the cause of David's music? Many of our best songs grow out of disappointment. Peter seemed to thrive on stress. However Jesus is our best example. No one ever lived under such awesome stress as He. Yet His inner peace, His balance, and His joy were apparent to all. Ironically, Judas Iscariot was destroyed by stress (Matt. 27:3-5).

Can I make stress my friend, or at least manage to avoid the damage it can bring? The answer is affirmative if I'm willing to make the effort, learn and practice the disciplines, and trust in God.

First, I must work, not at avoiding work but at making it play. Work, Selye contended, is what we *have* to do; play is what we *like* to do. Work is a basic biological need; to avoid it is to make life sterile and boring. What was it Sigmund Freud considered basic, necessary human functions? Work and love? We discover ourselves by discovering what we can do. None are so weary as those who never work enough to enjoy sleep, and hunger is always the best cook. If possible, find joy and satisfaction in your work.

Second, build up your resistance by good health habits: proper diet, regular exercise, and sleep. The healthy body makes stress easier to tolerate. Avoid debilitating drugs. When you feel good, you're more likely to keep things in balance.

Third, if you want to handle stress learn to laugh and play. Increasingly, therapists are discovering the healing that can come via laughter and play. Innovators, particularly on the West Coast, have developed play therapy for the release of pressure to be used in group dynamics. To participate in one of these groups is to see the release that can come to adults in returning almost to the innocence of childhood as they engage in simple and even ridiculous games.

Fourth, compartmentalize your work and nonwork life. Work hard on the job, but when you get home, blank out job problems. Especially, safeguard family meal time. Let this be a time of unadulterated pleasure. Enjoy your family, love your spouse, play with your children, and be fun to be around at home. A happy night at home will make tomorrow a better day.

Fifth, honor your feelings. Be honest about them. Get them out in the open. Find someone with whom you can share them. When you're angry, admit you're angry. When you feel you're being loaded with more than you can bear, tell someone about it. Never be like the guy who said, "I never get mad. I just get hurt." Maybe he could endure it but he drove everybody else crazy. Honor your feelings.

Sixth, minimize the insignificant, forget the pesky irritations, and accept the little hurts life brings. Everybody has them, why should you be exempt? Be yourself; keep your life as simple as possible. Choose to be as happy as you can be.

Finally, learn flexibility.

Hans Selye said before he died: "Although we were not a noble family, we had a family coat of arms and a motto that said, 'Related to few, but adaptable to everything.' "[2] He believed and proved in his own life that adaptability is the golden key to open the door to living productively in a stressful world.

Ways to Make Stress Your Friend

1. *Learn to play; it's not just for kids.*
2. *Pace yourself; you can't get it all done today.*
3. *Give yourself permission to be imperfect.*
4. *Guard your personal freedoms.*
5. *Give in once in a while.*
6. *Leave some things you can't handle to God.*

7 Ho Hum
Boredom

"Somebody's boring me . . . I think it's me."
—Dylan Thomas

Seated side by side in that typical American institution: the rocking chair, they gave the impression of serene contentment. After sixty years of marriage, they should feel relaxed. Pausing for a moment, he gazed at her, thinking how plain she looked. Then feeling guilty, he leaned over and said, "I'm proud of you." And she, not hearing correctly, responded, "I'm tired of you, too."

Are you exhausted, weary, and bored? Has life lost its zest? Do you find it hard to get up in the morning? What has caused this loss of energy, this listless indifference, this boredom? Are you ill, depressed, suffering from psychic burnout, loss of self-esteem, or too much defeat? Indeed, what causes boredom, and when are we most in danger from this debilitation emotion? How can we overcome it? How can we avoid it?

Eric Fromm, the psychologist-philosopher, argued that much of contemporary boredom has to do with what he called "consumerism" in modern industrial life. Long since most of us have been separated from the sources of production. Once, all people had to be producers to survive—cultivate and plant the seed, weed the fields, and bring in the harvest for food, build homes in which to live, make clothing, and provide diversions and entertainment, if there was to be any. Now most of us only consume. Most of us no longer grow the food we eat, make the clothes we wear, build the houses in which we live, or even entertain ourselves. We can purchase these things, and with economic affluence we may consume not because of needs but to impress, flaunt, amuse, and comfort. In due course we become satiated, filled to revulsion, and boredom becomes inevitable.

Perhaps our problem is aggravated by our affluence. Sometimes children at Christmas, for example, receive so many gifts they care for none. The problem of boredom is largely a problem of the affluent, for the poor are so preoccupied with survival they have little time to feel bored. The very fact that so many have both discretionary money and discretionary time—the luxury of excess—presents an enlarged potential for boredom.

Abundance can enrich life or become "superfluous." Fromm argued that *abundance* is a positive word having to do with possibilities for richness, fullness, and generosity but *superfluous* is negative implying waste, ostentation, and pointlessness. He said that ennui (languor) is even stronger than boredom, indicating disgust, dissatisfaction, that is, "to make loathsome and hateful." Has modern boredom become ennui? To consume and not produce, to receive and not give, to take and not share is to rob life of its primary functions. Even a young child knows how much more fun it is to make something than to receive something. We were made to create, produce, contribute, and be useful. Here is "the joy of functioning," the satisfaction of acting, the pleasure of contributing. Human beings are never fully themselves until they express themselves, until they make use of their powers within. Marie Montessori discovered children can be *trained* by the old system of rewards and punishments, but not *educated* with it. If you wish to teach, help your students do something you can affirm, approve, and find joy in.

Boredom is never cured by indulgence; indeed, more often it is caused by it. You came into this world to create, produce, contribute, and to utilize the powers within yourself. Want to conquer boredom? Then, get interested in something outside yourself of value and worth, and get busy! God said of His creation that it was very good and maybe one day you can say that of yours.

While, no doubt, Fromm was correct, our "consumerism" pattern of life is one cause of boredom, it is not the only cause, perhaps not even the major one. Many things contribute to boredom: the monotony and routine of one's work, lack of incentive and challenge, too much pressure over too long a period, unrealistic expectations, and the lack of meaning in so much of our work. Sometimes the cause is lack of imagination, sometimes not enough challenge, and sometimes not enough to do. Boredom has to do with loss of meaning, loss of challenge, and loss of joy.

How do we motivate each other to improve, grow, and be more productive? Charles Schwab, the man Andrew Carnegie employed to manage his far-flung steel empire, became legend in American business, partly because he was the first man in history to earn a million dollars a year, but even more because of his ability to motivate others. He once said there were many who knew more about producing steel than he, but his greatest asset was his ability to arouse enthusiasm among other men.[2]

He told of the mill manager whose men were not producing their quota of work. The manager had tried everything. It was near the end of the day, just as the day shift was leaving, and the night shift was coming on. "Give me a piece of chalk," Schwab said. Then turning to the nearest man he asked, "How many heats did your shift make today?" "Six." Without another word, Schwab took the chalk and wrote a big 6 on the floor. When the night shift came, they saw the 6 and asked what it meant. They decided they could do better. The next morning they erased the 6 and wrote 7. Day by day the production improved until the plant became the most productive in the company.[3]

Friendly competition, a sense of community, rewarding excellence often become an antidote to boredom.

What are the cures for boredom?

- Find the cause and do something about it.
- Accept the fact that the cause is more likely to be within us than outside us.
- Find something you enjoy doing, and do it.
- Associate with exciting people.
- Stretch yourself.
- Create an environment where failure is not fatal.
- Spend some time each week with someone who believes in you.
- Work at encouraging others.
- Stay active regardless of how you feel.
- Worship with joyful believers.
- Reject the critical spirit.

- Let love cover a multitude of sins.

Rabbi Harold S. Kushner (you remember his book: *Why Bad Things Happen to Good People*) suggested Ecclesiastes, which he called "the most dangerous book in the Bible," as an antidote to boredom.[4] If you think the suggestion strange, then read the biblical book. The biblical author, an honest, searching cynic, shared his own search for meaning in life. He began in the pit of gloom:

> "Meaningless! Meaningless!" says the Teacher.
> "Utterly meaningless! Everything is meaningless."
> What does man gain from all his labor
> at which he toils under the sun?
> Generations come and generations go,
> but the earth remains forever (Eccl. 1:2-4, NIV).

The opening verses would convince us that we're born in pain, struggle, grow, labor, suffer, grow old, die, and are forgotten—or that there is no ultimate meaning to our existence. But our writer was not convinced, for the whole book is a continuation of argument. Indeed, he told us in painful detail of his struggle.

He began by determining the values most admired by his age: wealth, pleasure, wisdom, asceticism, and traditional piety. Then he set out to achieve them, one by one, and to personally determine how much real satisfaction each would bring. He made money, lots of it. He indulged the appetites of the flesh. He pursued wisdom. He even took a turn at traditional piety. But none of them gave meaning to his life. The Teacher had one thing on most of us: he made enough money and had enough pleasure to know that these things, in themselves, are not enough.

Most of us have never made enough money to be sure having a million dollars wouldn't give meaning to our lives. Our words are not always consistent with our dreams. Money, pleasure, and wisdom do not finally satisfy; however, millions of people are not as convinced as the author of Ecclesiastes was.

However, the futility of satisfying our souls with things is not the only lesson of this book. Read Ecclesiastes 9:7-10. Here we discover our biblical author was more than a cynic. Listen to his counsel as interpreted by Rabbi Kushner:

> "Go eat your bread in gladness and drink your wine in joy, for your action was long ago approved by God." Here is God's commandment to joy. We were created for beauty, celebration, exuberance, joy—these are the purposes of our being. There is meaning in the laughter of a child, the melody of a song, the radiance of a sunset. Do you recall that ancient Talmudic text? "In the world to come, each of us will be called to account for all the good things God put on earth which we've refused to enjoy."[5]

Doesn't that include food and hunger, work and rest, excitement and pleasure, marital intimacy and sex, prayer and praise? This is a good world created by a God of love for our use and joy. The ancient preacher continued: "Let your clothes always be freshly washed and your head never lack ointment. Enjoy happiness with a woman you love." The counsel is explicit, full of imagery, difficult to misunderstand. The preacher's final word is the most important of all: "Whatever it is your power to do, do it with all your might." Here is life lived for its own sake, the pleasure that comes in giving our best to every undertaking.

Why is it that most of us assume that the purpose of life lies in reaching goals, moving to certain levels, and remaining there? Is it because we were taught that in our childhood? "When you grow up, when you finish school, when you get a job"—we were admonished over and over until we come to feel this was the purpose of our living. Then we received that diploma or got that job, and while it brought satisfaction, life did not stop there. Life is living every day, every moment—challenge, opportunity, pleasure, movement, growth, and becoming. "Whatsoever thy hand findeth to do, do it with thy might." There's a text to fight boredom.

Of course, Ecclesiastes, as true and moving as it is, is not the final answer. We must add Jesus and the gospel. Antonio Stradivari, the Italian who crafted the best violins made on earth, said, "I make violins to the glory of God." We can live to the glory of God, and "the joy of Lord" can chase away the gloom of boredom.

A Cure for Boredom

1. *Find the cause.*
2. *Don't complain.*
3. *Share with a friend.*
4. *Do something.*
5. *Trust God.*

8   Caught in a Trap
Enslaving Habits

"No man can be free who is not master of himself."
—Epictetus

We live by our habits: that complex and enigmatic web of behavior responses we make to the stimuli we receive every day. These responses are largely learned in childhood, and they are necessary for our survival and peace of mind. Otherwise, we'd be debating constantly our reactions to the endless sequence of sensations that come our way. Without these patterns of response, we might literally ride off in all directions all the time. In a sense, maturity is learning to live by healthy, wholesome, and satisfying patterns of habit.

Perhaps these patterns of behavior begin in response to bodily needs such as hunger, thirst, elimination, rest, affection, and to the devices we use to meet these needs. As an infant, we learn the actions necessary to get the attention and care from other people we need and want. Sometimes the patterns we learn are healthy, pleasant, and satisfying both to ourselves and others, but sometimes they are not. Responses, if continued long enough, become a fixed pattern, an automatic response, and a habit, ingrained and difficult to modify. Little by little these habits accumulate, and in time become the structure of our manner of living.

Happiness has been defined as "living by the right habits," misery as "caught in the web of the wrong ones." But there is, I think, a manner of living superior to both. The Bible calls it "abundant life," a state where the better self is free to live by the image of God stamped within us, a Spirit-enabled life, dominated by love, which is open to generosity and joy, work and play, intimacy and worship, growth and change, exuberance and celebration. In this quality of life, habits are balanced by free choice.

In one of the Gospels, there is a remarkable insight recorded about Jesus. The Gentile physician, Luke, set it down for us. "And he came to Nazareth, where he had been brought up: and, as his custom was, he went into the synagogue on the sabbath day" (Luke 4:16). From the account, it is obvious the synagogue was not always a godly place, and our Lord radically disagreed with much that was taught there, yet from childhood he had honored the human need for worship. "As his custom was," that is, as His pattern of habits directed Him. What are your good habits? Patterns of behavior that bring pleasure and satisfaction to you, your family, your neighbors, your friends, and your community? How do we strengthen such habits and multiply them, especially how do we keep open our options to modify and improve our habits as the years pass?

There are evil habits that damage and destroy life. Do you recall that strange verse in the first book of the Bible about Cain and the murder of his brother, Abel? "If thou doest not well, sin lieth at the door" (Gen. 4:7*b*). What did the ancient narrator have in mind? That anger, uncontrolled and habitual, becomes a wild beast, tensed, alert, waiting to spring and devour the personality? Was this the first example of sibling rivalry? Why did Cain do what he did? Did he feel neglected, spurned, unappreciated, threatened, or cornered?

Why do we do the things we do? First our feelings play havoc with our imaginations, then our minds, overwhelmed by our emotions, begin the process of rationalization, and soon our deeds are justified. Our deeds, good or bad, become habits, and habits make our lives. We are all caught in the web of habits, some beneficent and healthy, others destructive and misery producing. But the most deadly of all are those which enslave us and catch us in a trap from which there is no escape. Is there an escape?

Have you ever thought about grading tyrants, the people and forces which enslave human beings? There are many, as all of us know: habits, experiences, patterns of behavior, clever advertisers appealing to our baser instincts, and the less noble instinctual forces within us. But of all such tyrants, the most deadly, particularly in our social climate, are the *chemicals* we choose to take into our bodies, which in due course, so absorb us that we determine we cannot live without them. Yet, ironically, these chemicals which often destroy can have beneficent usages. Drugs are indispensable in the practice of medicine. Yet we live in a society where drug abuse is wreaking havoc.

Four major drug groups are used in our society: hallucinogenic (marijuana, hashish, LSD), depressants (Nembutal, Luminal, Equanil, Librium), stimulants (cocaine, Benzedrine, Dexedrine, Methedrine), and narcotics (opium, morphine). Many of these are relatively new discoveries in the long history of humankind, and they have many beneficent uses. Who can imagine complicated surgery without drugs? Yet their misuse has become the curse of the Western world.

If you have doubts about the above conclusion then ask one of the estimated 22 million alcoholics[1] (20 million practicing and 2 million in recovery) and the 110 million (5 for each alcoholic) family members and friends affected. I have chosen alcohol because, though more widely used and socially approved, it represents a major social problem. Drugs are chemical substances—solid, liquid, or gaseous—which when used by an individual alter the state of consciousness.

While no way has been found to predict who will become addicted, the more euphoric (pleasurable) the reaction, the greater the danger. Dr. Arthur H. Cain, psychologist, counselor, and author, warning of the danger, wrote of a personal experience in participating in a professionally controlled experiment:

> I had just enough reaction to understand with piercing clarity how easy it would be to become addicted to this most powerful . . . insidious of drugs. The experience was unbelievable euphoric (pleasurable), and I knew absolutely that if I experienced it even one more time I would continue to try to capture the sensation.[2]

Why this euphoria comes to some and not others is as yet inexplainable, but that it does is a verifiable fact, and the greater the euphoria, the greater the danger of addiction.

Perhaps you ask the differences between addiction and

dependency. In our use, there are none. They are interchangeable, and the problems of addiction are identical regardless of the addicting agent. Addiction or dependency contribute to the same ultimate anguish and pain. Increasingly, with the proliferation of chemicals, more and more addicts are using multiple drugs.

Among all enslaving habits, none are so devastating and insidious as chemical addiction, particularly for the young. Tragically, thousands are addicted in childhood and youth, some even while in their mother's womb. The most frequent reply Mrs. Ronald Reagan gets to her question: "What turned you on?" when she visits addiction centers, is, "My parents."[3] As incredible as it sounds, there are parents who give infants alcohol to stop their crying, and even for amusement to watch their reaction. Most teenagers who drink and take drugs start by the time they reach the seventh grade.

What can be done about this problem?

First, we will consider the plight of the chemically addicted person. This is the most enslaving habit of all. Chemical dependency is the most brutal and complex tyranny known. The drug-dependent person is governed totally by the focus of his addiction, and in turn he governs others totally. He becomes an awesome tyrant who in time alters the thoughts, feelings, and behavior of those around him: spouses, lovers, parents, and children who often believe they have no other choice. The onset of the chemically dependent person's control is subtle, and before the family knows it, he or she is caught. Often the dependent's illness is sporadic, and the family assumes improvement has come.

Ruth Maxwell, in her book *Breakthrough,* reassures

family members, "You're not crazy although you are repeatedly told you are." She contends there are three patterns in every addicted household: (1) The drug-addicted person is the most important person in the family. His or her needs and wants matter most. (2) The drug-addicted person is always right. No matter what you do, you never win. (3) The alcohol or drug use is not the primary problem.[4]

The terrible tragedy of drug addiction is the loss of control. Free will is gone. Drunk or sober, drugged or clean, addiction becomes the dominating force in the person's whole perspective. His autonomy disappears. Eventually, the drug destroys his integrity, his honor, and his sense of values. His mind plays tricks on him as he does and says things to secure the drug which now has him enslaved. In this sense he is ill, for he cannot stop or control it. And he has to use ever larger amounts to get the desired effect. Ironically, no one ever starts out wanting to become an alcoholic or drug addict.

Our purpose in this chapter is not to deal with all the facets of the drug-addiction problem. (There are a growing number of excellent books on the subject.) But we will point out some ways to help you make it through the day. Do you have a husband, wife, parent, or child who is chemically dependent? What do you do?

- *You reverse what you've been doing:* You stop trying to control the chemical use; you can't make the addict do what he can't do. You stop advising, warning, and reasoning knowing the addict is beyond logic. You start thinking of yourself, your needs and wants, not his.

- *You unload the guilt, anger, resentment, and sense of failure you've been piling on yourself.*
- *You stop asking yourself, how can I make him stop?* You can't. You accept reality. You abuse yourself of the fantasy: all he needs is love.
- *You don't show your love by enabling, lying, letting off.* You don't become a codependent.
- *You may feel it wise to force intervention.* Reality plus love are hard to beat. Planned intervention can do for the dependent what he cannot do for himself, and he does not have to agree to it. But you need professional counsel and others to assist you.
- *You can't make feelings go away. Deal with them.*
- *Take hope.* While you can't heal the person, there are millions of recovered alcoholics.
- *Let go of handling it alone.*
- *When the addict stops, it won't be the same.* Find other interests.
- *Open yourself to God's love and the love of others.*

Finally, how does the chemically addicted person make it through the day, indeed improve and change the day?

- *Admit the problem and accept responsibility for it.* Stop blaming other people.
- *Come clean. Lay it on the line. Tell it like is. And do it while you're still rational and able to do so.* I can almost hear him now. He had permitted drug dependency to alienate his children, almost destroy his wife, and damage his health. Finally cornered, he had entered treatment. Everybody but him knew he needed treatment, and he fought it as if tormented. But notwithstanding, he made it, and I recall his

report: "For the first time I admitted I had a disease,
and I couldn't do a thing about it. It had made me
into a monster who blamed everybody but myself. I
don't know how I brought myself to do it, but in
listening to others, I got the courage to tell mine, lies
and all. They kicked me in the pants and made me
see it was my problem, not my wife's or my parents'
or my job's. I was the b _ _ _ _ _ _ and I admitted it.
Finally, I admitted I was powerless when it came to
alcohol, but there was a Power outside me, greater
than me, and I had to turn my life over to Him. I had
to confess to the world my failures and His deliver-
ance." I have never forgotten that confession, and I
can still see the light in my friend's eyes.

- *Whatever your addiction: tobacco, food, spending
money, or speeding in automobiles, you need help. You
must find something to take its place, and you must
do it one day at a time.*

- *Remember the ancient promise, "As many as received
him, to them gave the power to become the sons of
God"* (John 1:12, author's italics). To as many as
receive Him, He still gives power. The receiving involves learning, submitting, and obeying. "Spiritual
growth is the bedrock, the foundation from which all
else proceeds in chemical dependency treatment."[5]
Drug addiction shrivels the spirit, and to be set free
is to be released to begin growth again toward "the
measure of the stature of the fulness of Christ" (Eph.
4:13).

Do You Want to Be Set Free?

1. *Admit you're enslaved.*
2. *Come clean. Lay it on the line.*
3. *Stop blaming other people.*
4. *Express your emotions.*
5. *Get help.*
6. *Share your victory.*

9 "I'm Sorry—I Forgive You"
Forgiveness

"To be wronged or robbed is nothing unless you remember it."

—Confucius

Some believe forgiveness is our deepest human need. Mother Teresa, working with the poorest of the poor on the streets of Calcutta, told of rescuing an old lady, dying in a garbage bin where her son had put her, who simply would not permit herself to die until she knew her son had forgiven her, although she had been the one sinned against. The chief obstetrical nurse in a large New York City hospital reports that women in the pains of labor, regardless of background or faith, have one common expression: "Lord, have mercy." All of us long to know we are forgiven by God and others, and all of us need to forgive ourselves and others.

Even a two-year-old apparently with no sense of sin, after he has disobeyed, comes seeking forgiveness. An eight-year-old once gave me my best definition of forgiveness: "It means your Mamma treats you like you hadn't done it." The barrier to love had been removed; he belonged again. Once in our childhood my sister and I, in the absence of our parents, had a broom battle with a glass door between us. Although both of us contended neither was at fault, we both wanted forgiveness. Forgiveness won't restore the broken glass or undo the damage the deed has done, but it will mend the relationship. How we long for that restoration!

However, forgiveness is never cheap—either for us or for God. Indeed, forgiving love may be the costliest thing in the universe. Confession, repentance, restitution—these are not just biblical terms but principles of human psychology and life. Until we accept responsibility for ourselves, relationships have little or no meaning, and this very responsibility is what makes forgiveness necessary.

Do you have problems with forgiveness? Which kind of forgiveness, you might ask: Forgiving myself, or forgiving others? "I'm sorry. Please forgive me." There you have one side of forgiveness. But there is the other side, "You hurt me, but I forgive you." Who can say which is more difficult? Yet both are necessary if life is to be satisfying, useful, and joyful. Confessing my faults or tolerating yours? Handling resentment or living with my own imperfections? So much of life is bound up in the two questions.

"The only perfect man I ever knew," the man confessed with a twinkle in his eye, "was my wife's first husband!" We know we're not perfect, but not many of us enjoy confessing it. "I've heard my father pray many times," the young woman sitting in my office confessed, "but I've never heard him admit a fault, even to God." When you're wrong, can you admit it to your spouse, your child, or your associate? How often when we're angry with ourselves, we take it out on those we love. When you're angry talk, about *your* feelings, not others' faults. Let others respond. Ventilate but not annihilate. Balance criticism with affection. Anger can arise because of care, but let it serve love rather than destroy love.

Often our problem in confessing our faults lies in some image we have of ourselves planted in our minds in childhood: a parent said over and over, "Be nice, be strong, be good, don't cry." Or we imagined admitting a fault was a sign of weakness or foolishness. Do males have more difficulty here than females? Do you need to say to yourself: "I don't have to be perfect to be loved; I don't have to compete to be valued; I don't have to dominate to be admired; I don't have to act tough to be strong." Indeed, you may destroy your marriage, your home, or your career if you do not learn that people who are loved admit their imperfections.

Her face was drawn and dark, her eyes filled with tears, her lips quivered as she tried to speak, and her fingers seemed to move endlessly as if reaching for something that was not there. She had sounded desperate when she called, alluding to depression and suicide. She had asked if I could see her. Ten minutes later she walked in my office door.

Haltingly, she began her story. Every sentence seemed to be extracted with agonizing pain. Her sins were so great she wanted to die. Indeed, over and over, she said she deserved to die. She had been thinking of suicide all day. Finally, she got her story out. She was the eldest child of poor parents; she had known only deprivation and strain all her years. There were ten other children, and her father knew nothing of human psychology. He ridiculed her dreams, spoiled her ideals, and could not understand her desires. More and more she came to hate him, until one day she began to pray he would die, and he did. Soon her guilt was unendurable, and she drove herself to desperation.

I listened to every detail of her story, reminded her that her feelings and prayers concerning her father would not have caused his death, assured her that I understood, and so did God; I tried as best I could to imprint on her mind and feelings the limitless forgiveness and love of God. But each time I sought to reassure her, she would cry out in anguish, "But you don't understand! I *prayed* for him to die!"

Finally I asked if she believed the Bible, and when she assured me she did, we read together 1 John 1:8 to 2:2. Over and over we read it, discussed it, prayed about it, and claimed it. I can see her now after all these years, as she arose from her knees, wiped her tear-stained cheeks, and walked out of my study into the afternoon sunlight. As she straightened her stooped shoulders and walked away, I thought of Mary Magdalene on resurrection morning.

Do you find it difficult to forgive yourself? Many do. First, confront your sins with honesty and candor. Genuine self-forgiveness, if it is to bring inner cleansing and peace, will not come from being casual about your faults. You can't earn God's forgiveness: that is pure grace. But you must earn you own inner self-respect. You repent, confess, make restitution where possible, and you accept God's love and forgiveness. Dr. Hobart Mowrer with his "reality therapy" contended that until we accept personal responsibility for our own behavior, as long as we live under the shadow of real, yet unacknowledged and unexpiated guilt, we hate ourselves, and have little cleansing or peace. We "come clean" with ourselves and God and leave our sins at the cross. God, who is love, does not want any mortal to live with unforgiven sin, plagued by guilt, despising self, and estranged from others.

Then rejoice in your cleansing and forgiveness, remembering Charles Wesley's promise: "He breaks the pow'r of canceled sin, He sets the pris'ner free." Rejoice in that freedom, claim it, and live by it. Make a list of the grudges you hold against yourself. The things you dislike but do, the things you wish you never did. Is your list like mine?

- I hate my loose tongue.
- I abhore my compulsive anxiety.
- Why do I lose my cool?
- Show me how to be confident, unafraid, and relaxed.

Take them to God. Ask Him to show you why you do them, how to believe in yourself, how to rejoice in His love for you, and in the joy of that discovery you will begin to break your obsession with your faults. His grace will help you break "the pow'r of canceled sin."

Confessing our faults and asking for forgiveness when we are wrong is the healthiest and happiest way, even if not always the easiest, but there's the other side of forgiveness: What we do when we're mistreated? Do we yield to resentment or even violence, or do we love our enemies, turn the other cheek, and forgive?

Again the choice is not easy. When we're affronted, insulted, humiliated, and injured, anger nearly always rises within us. We feel sheer justice requires retaliation, and in that irrational moment there may be a strange sort of pleasure in settling the score. How often devastating actions are taken before rationality returns. Why do I resent politicians, tax collectors, oil companies, free lovers, my in-laws, or the boss? They use me, threaten me, abuse me, cause me inconvenience, and devalue me. Of course, sometimes it's all in my mind. Sometimes the injuries we receive are trivial and slight, and sometimes they are devastating and terrible. Nothing demonstrates immaturity more dramatically than hypersensitivity to small slights. However there are terrible and tragic injuries inflicted by human beings on other human beings.

In her book: *And I Am Afraid of My Dreams,* Wanda Poltanka, a Polish psychiatrist imprisoned in Ravensbruck at nineteen and used for brutal medical and surgical experiments, tells how former victims, now old, are plagued by nightmares from those years of trauma. In many ways there is no healing as long as one lives. Dr. Poltanka tells how she could not erase hatred for the innocent red hostas whose bright red beds were so orderly and beautiful at Ravensbruck. Today she avoids them because they bring back such painful memories. Ravensbruck was Corrie Ten Boom's final prison, and her struggle to forgive could be a pattern and inspiration to all who are brutalized by others.

Do you recall the rationale Jesus gives for His command to His followers to "Love your enemies"? "That ye may be the children of your Father which is in heaven: for he maketh his sun to rise on the evil and on the good, and sendeth rain on the just and on the unjust" (Matt. 5:45). "Like father, like child." It's an old proverb which should mark the lives of believers. Jesus had a radically new definition of neighbor that astonished the religious leaders of His day. The rabbis had always been moved by the sheer beneficence of God to saint and sinner alike but had never imagined such love possible between mortals. Here is something new, wonderful, and revolutionary.

What does love have to do with resentment? We can resent not just mistreatment from others but our circumstances in life. Perhaps self-pity is the ultimate resentment. People can resent God, themselves, their families, and everybody else. How does love cure resentment? Not by concentrating on feelings, as important as they are. Not by feeding guilt for self-inflicted punishment which never brings release. Not by mere resolution or positive thinking alone. Love is energy that finds its source in God and multiplies by becoming active in the world. Love is both a gift and an achievement, and we learn it at the cross. We begin by rejoicing in our own forgiveness, and we discover a life-style that has a way of lifting the believer above resentment.

How can we handle resentment?

We can talk it out. Canned resentment can be like a hidden explosive waiting to go off. It can cause both physical and emotional illness. "Talking it out" can be a *catharsis* (a Greek word meaning purging or cleansing). We can "blow off steam," an apt phrase, which can sometimes be literally true. However in consideration of those we love, we must set limits or get professional help.

We can work it off. Even ancient people knew physical exercise could discharge high energy generated by irritation, anger, and resentment. Were you ever so angry, you kicked the chair (on which you had stumbled)? It was a silly thing to do, but if the chair were not too expensive and you didn't break your toe, it brought some relief. With furniture so expensive, I don't recommend it, but nonetheless relieving an emotion with action is a sound psychological principle. Some people use a punching bag, some put select names on golf or tennis balls, and other people use rugs. All of these are better than hitting a person.

We can use understanding and imagination. Try to figure out the emotion that triggered the affront. Ask yourself why you resent it, and what you can do about it. Ask yourself why the same thing when done by a stranger seems no affront, but when done by someone you love can be devastating. Creative imagination may discover new ways of forgiving, relating, and loving.

We can let God's love flow through us. Only love can change an enemy into a friend. Examine ways God has worked in your life in the past. Open the doors, remove the barriers, and give grace a chance. Pray for those who mistreat you.

Jonathan Edwards may have possessed the most brilliant mind in Colonial America. He was born in a tiny Connecticut village, educated at Yale for the ministry, and stepped into his grandfather's church at Northampton, Massachusetts, as pastor at twenty-six. Five years later he was famous. The whole Western world was talking about him. Then a brief ten years later, everything had gone wrong; that was in 1744. By 1750, the opposition was so great that the church voted to dismiss the famous pastor. With a wife and ten children, Edwards tried to find work and failed. The church, in the meantime, failed to find a minister and invited him to supply for them until they could locate a pastor. Imagine preaching in a pulpit where the people, a few months previously, had voted to oust you. But Edwards controlled his feelings and served until the next year when he was called to Stockbridge, a tiny town with limited opportunity. Here he preached and wrote four theological treatises that mark him as one of the most original thinkers America has produced.

When resentment is your problem, think of Jonathan Edwards and Jesus!

Tips to Remember

1. *Everybody makes mistakes. Admit them and ask for forgiveness.*
2. *Expect mistreatment and keep it in perspective.*
3. *Refuse to let resentment dominate your life.*
4. *Let love cure your resentment.*

10   Be Anxious in Nothing
Anxiety

"Life is a banquet, and so many are starving; a party, and so many are sad."

—Anonymous

We have been called "the champion insomniacs of the world," and perhaps we deserve the reputation. Obsessed with deadlines, always in a hurry, aggressive and competitive, we seem addicted to wanting more and always trying to prove ourselves. "You Americans invented the rocking chair," my European friend declares, "so you could keep moving while you sit still." Our life-styles contribute to anxiety. Did you ever wonder how many billions of headaches we have each year, and how many tons of pain relievers we consume? Our hospitals are filled with people suffering from stress-related diseases. When filled with anxiety, we have little room left for enjoyment.

"When a day is finished, I leave it," my father used to say. And he meant it. Perhaps he overdid it, for he rarely put away his tools, but then he was wiser than so many who, while they would never say, "When a day is finished, I worry about it," lived that way all the time. Anxiety might be termed a national disease.

Anxiety is a composite of feelings: apprehension, dread, terror, and nervousness. These all are products of worried thinking. To an amazing degree we create the stresses that plague us. All of us talk to ourselves, but our conversation centers on negative factors rather than positive ones. We focus on feelings rather than tasks and permit our emotion to affect our bodies, and in turn these physical symptoms convince our minds. We find ourselves caught in a vicious cycle. In a helpful book: *Stress, Sanity and Survival,* Woolfolk and Richardson pointed out three characteristics of worry which most of us rarely consider:

1. Worry is self-escalating.
2. Worry is self-perpetuating.
3. Worry is self-oriented.

Worry feeds on itself, and by its very nature, it has a tendency to balloon. One bad report invites another, and for some perverse reason, worriers seem determined to make things worse and worse. Not only does worry feed on itself, it escalates, and like the many-headed dragon becomes increasingly difficult to slay.

Woolfolk and Richardson also listed four categories of beliefs which lie at the root of most anxiety. They are (1) a belief in the efficacy of worry, (2) our tendency to measure our self-worth by performance standards, (3) our assumptions that a loss of relationships can destroy all possibilities for happiness, and (4) the widely held belief, even among successful people, that they are in some way inferior or disadvantaged.[2] Examine the basis of your anxiety. You will be surprised how often one or more of the above is involved.

Most of us were taught as children that if we are to

succeed we must be aggressive, determined, and tense. Our parents warned us about the danger of being too relaxed and casual. We didn't call it anxiety, but we felt we must be that way if we were to please those who loved us and to make our way in the world. Without knowing it, we were taught to believe in the efficacy of worry.

"The birthright of every American," someone has said, "is a constant sense of personal inadequacy." "I'm not good enough." "I ought to be better." You've heard them all your life. Where do they come from? Our Puritan ethic, a morbid sense of guilt, a penchant for putting ourselves down? Our proclivity to equate our self-worth with our performance? This is one of the reasons a career failure can be so devastating, particularly to the American male. Sometimes professional success is equated with proof of love. Such an assumption guarantees anxiety. The same is true when we assume that any loss in relationship will destroy emotional security. Actually, no relationship can provide a basis for self-esteem or self-confidence. No other person can guarantee our self-esteem or make it possible for us to love ourselves. As long as we try to deny these facts of life we are vulnerable to anxiety. The same, of course, is true when we assume there is some defect in us that makes it difficult for us to live a satisfying life. Most of our anxiety is grounded in these four false assumptions.

Let me give you a prescription for anxiety:

- Assume worry is necessary.
- Feel yourself unworthy.
- Make yourself overly dependent on other people.
- Regard yourself as inferior.

- Overidentify with too many people, too many things, too many ideas, and too many causes.
- See yourself as a custodian of public morals.
- Be competitive with win-lose attitudes.
- Attribute your negative thinking to other people.
- Assume you have a right to happiness.
- Be a perfectionist.

In learning to conquer anxiety we need understanding, but we also need faith: faith in God, faith in ourselves, faith in life's meaning and purpose. Years ago I had a friend, an uneducated laboring man who told me once the secret of his serenity. "When things get out of hand, I red letter them!" When I asked for an explanation, he said when he couldn't figure out what to do, he took a red letter edition of the New Testament (the words of Jesus printed in red type) and read until he found his answer. Would you be insulted if I suggested we "red letter" this problem of anxiety? Jesus said, "Take no thought for your life, what shall ye eat; . . . what ye shall put on. . . . The life is more than meat, and the body is more than raiment" (Luke 12:22 *ff.*). May I paraphrase the passage?

Don't be anxious about your breath, your health, or what you wear. Life is more than food or clothes or even breath. Consider the birds; take sparrows, for example, they neither sow nor reap, have no barns or granaries, yet God feeds them. Are you not of more value in God's eye than sparrows? And what good will your anxiety do? Do you think it can add five minutes to your life? If you can't manage a thing like that why worry about the rest? Consider the wild flowers. They neither weave nor work. They have no dyer's vats nor clothes designers, yet even

Solomon was not dressed like one of them. If God makes the grass grow, verdant and beautiful one day and burned in the oven as fuel the next, how much more will He clothe you? Oh, you little faiths, stop setting your hearts on what you eat and drink and wear; neither be harassed with life's cares, for these are the very things an unbelieving world seeks. Don't you think God knows you need these things?

Sometimes I have to read these words over and over before they filter down into my emotions. My anxieties refuse to listen. Sometimes, I line my emotions up and lecture to them, and after a while they begin to hear.

These words of Jesus tell us five things we need to hear:

1. *When God loves us, why be anxious?* If God gives us lives to be fed and bodies to be clothed, do we imagine He will permit us to starve or freeze? There is nothing here to encourage indolence, lack of foresight, or restraint of industry. Our Lord takes all of these for granted. Nor is there a promise of luxury or indulgence. There is simply the assurance that if we do our part, God will do His, and the prohibition against living lives full of anxiety and care.

2. *Consider the birds.* The birds are provided for. God feeds them. They don't fret and worry, but they work. Few men work as hard for their living as a sparrow. "God spends every year in feeding sparrows more than the revenues of the king of France," Martin Luther once observed. Look out your window, watch the birds, and learn from them the lesson of trust. When you've done your best, leave the rest with God.

3. *What good will your anxiety do?* Your anxiety serves no useful purpose. You can't extend your height or lengthen your days by worry. You may shorten your days by it.

Worry does not empty tomorrow of its difficulties; it merely empties today of its strength. As Dean Inge put it: "Worry is interest paid on trouble before it comes due."

4. *Consider the wild flowers.* Life is full of tragedy but also full of serendipity! Are wild flowers part of what I call "life's extras"? All of us see the rationality of air and sunlight, of potatoes and wheat and corn, or bone and flesh and blood, but pray, tell me, why God made wild flowers? There is but one answer: He is a God of love. "They toil not, they spin not" (v. 27). They do neither men's nor women's work, yet even a Solomon, in his most flamboyant robes, suffers in comparison. One wild violet is more convincing than all Voltaire's atheism. Long ago John Duncan wrote:

> There are times when I cannot rest in the ethical, when I cannot find any satisfaction in historical facts. The very evangels satisfy me not. I cannot read my Bible, I cannot pray. But I go to my garden and consider the lilies.

5. *Don't act like a pagan.* Worry about material things is characteristic of pagan cultures, societies dominated by secular values, people who do not believe in a loving God. Here is the cause of much of our anxiety: we profess to believe in God, but we worship other things such as wealth, power, possessions, and status. Unsatisfied and disillusioned, rather than examining our goals, we redouble our efforts. Our confused values feed our anxieties and shorten our lives. Lin Yutang said, "Only those who take leisurely what the people of the world are busy about, can be busy about what the world takes leisurely."

Make a list of all the things that cause you anxiety. Be candid and specific. Leave nothing out. Let your list be exhaustive. Admit and express your honest feelings. Next find positive ways of addressing them. Here are my ways:

- *Look them straight in the eye and determine what causes them.* Sometimes the causes are real and awesome. "My father, who is in his fifties, has received notice his company no longer needs his services. I have two sisters still in college, and my mother isn't well. He's devastated." Of course he is! "We've just learned our teenage daughter is pregnant." "My business is headed for bankruptcy." "The tests came back malignant." "I know of no way to save our marriage." These are tragedies and cannot be wished away, and you'd be foolish to take them casually. For some of them, there are no perfect solutions. You have no choice but to face reality, evaluate your choices, come to terms with what you cannot change, act decisively, and accept God's forgiveness and grace and move on.

- *Next, you ask yourself what would be the worst possible scenario?* If the worst possible option became a reality, what would it mean? You'd lose your job, be embarrassed, go to jail, or get reprimanded? When once you face up to your fears, you can tolerate them with less anxiety. Fears that are faced are less formidable. Facing one's fears is a source of freedom.

- *Then work them out rather than sigh them out.* Don't bottle up your anxieties, hide them in your loneliness, press them down into your unconscious mind. Share them with someone you can trust. Then, if you can, do something about them. If not, get yourself preoccupied with some other worthwhile activity.

- *When the day is finished, leave it.* My father was wiser than I thought.

A Cure for Anxiety

Be careful for nothing; but in every thing by prayer and supplication with thanksgiving let your requests be made known unto God. And the peace of God, which passeth all understanding, shall keep your hearts and minds through Christ Jesus (Phil. 4:6-7),

11   I Can't Help It!
Compulsiveness

"My mind says, 'No,' my feelings say, 'Yes.' Guess who wins?"

—Anonymous

Compulsive behavior, acting in ways I neither approve nor can rationalize, is as widespread as it is injurious. Obsessive, driven, and irrational—at times all of us do things we neither understand nor desire. *Why we do them?* we ask ourselves over and over. Motivation may be complex and unrecognized. I eat, not because I'm hungry but because I feel neglected, bored, or frustrated, and then I'm surprised to find myself overweight. I spend my money, not because I need merchandise—or even find satisfaction in having it—but to get attention, express anger, or reassure myself. I talk on and on not to communicate or express love but because I'm anxious, insecure, and obsessed. In all these cases, my behavior is compulsive.

Compulsiveness can be expressed in almost endless ways: drinking, driving, sleeping, exercising, gardening, jogging, traveling, working, criticizing, complimenting, manipulating, and even in praying. Any behavior that becomes an end in itself is compulsive. Any human action over which we have lost rational control becomes compulsive and is a source of embarrassment, misery, and perhaps pain. A careful, objective analysis of why we do what we do can be both surprising and embarrassing.

Take something all of us do every day: eating. Despite our contrary assumptions, we (particularly those of us living in the Western world) rarely eat only because we are hungry. Most overweight people who come to physicians for help admit their eating precedes their hunger. We eat for many reasons: force of habit, to be sociable, because of the psychic or physiological pleasures we receive, as a substitute for sex, attention, love, or to avoid sex, because we're bored or angry or neglected, and because of insomnia. The reasons are almost endless.

Why, then, are most of us overweight? Simply because our unconscious minds are programmed to believe that no matter what the problem, food will make us feel better. Let's face it: eating is a pleasure, a primal gratification, something that feels good, and a natural tranquilizer. Eating, an oral gratification we learned before we could think, was used to comfort, reward, and affirm us. Why shouldn't we enjoy eating? It was a token of love both from our families and those outside. You see, we must reprogram our emotional computer banks that keep us captive to the kitchen if we are to control our eating. Change your mind (or should I say emotions) to change your life, and you can also change your body.

How do you do it, you ask? You get medical help if you need it. That is taken for granted, but with most of us, illness isn't the real problem. We must find out why we overeat. Some eat when they're under pressure, some because they haven't learned to handle emotional stress.

They chew their problems. As someone observed, "To swallow your feelings will make you fat." I must be honest —perhaps ruthlessly honest with myself and candid. I must be prepared to admit to myself why I am compulsive.

Then to reprogram yourself, you must choose to lose weight; you must see the advantages, pleasures, and joys in doing so. You must have a strong, emotional motivator: one you can verify in your thinking, repeat in your memory, and verify in your feelings. You may also need negative reinforcers. One friend, who while compulsive about eating where I may be compulsive about talking, gave me her negative reasoning. First, fat people are thought lazy. Second, they're considered dumb. Third, they're thought careless. Finally, they're seen as ugly. When I protested she was being unfair, she said, "You've got to have a reason to lose weight. Most people who diet don't have it. They're casual. I'm desperate." By the way, she conquered her problem. Whatever your motive there must be a positive charge, a personal reason, and emotional energy involved. Is the motive better health, more energy, self-respect, or to look younger? Whatever it is, you must be certain you want it both with your mind and your heart. Put words to your feelings. Reward yourself and do it often. Only goodness overcomes evil, only positive emotions are powerful enough to conquer negative ones. Major on loving yourself rather than hating yourself.

Are you a compulsive smoker? Giving up cigarettes is not the way to stop smoking. The only permanent way is to convert yourself into a nonsmoker. You stop smoking because you no longer have the urge: you put something more positive and satisfying in its place. But you don't do it by simply making a resolution. First, you admit to yourself you really don't want to quit. You get gratification, pleasure, and good feelings from it. If you don't face it, your emotions will overwhelm your reasoning. Then you find an emotionally charged reason for not smoking. You must know what the payoff is both physically and psychologically. Then during the painful transition time, concentrate on the long-range rewards. The reward must offer emotional satisfaction. Train yourself, your subconscious, to say, "I'm proud to be a nonsmoker" every time someone lights up.

Of all our compulsions, perhaps none is so ironic as our human penchant to compulsive talking. "She shifted her brain into neutral and idled on." "He could take longer to say less than any man I ever knew." All of us understand these quips, for we live in a world of words. He was sixteen months old with bright blue eyes, a persistent smile, and no fear of strangers. When you came in the room, he'd walk up to you, look you in the eye, and begin to jabber with perfect body language as if every word were as clear as crystal. The child was adorable, but then he had not yet learned an intelligible language, and he could be forgiven. But so many who know better talk endlessly, say nothing, and finally cause much weariness of the flesh. In our years of marriage, we've had one neighbor who could call, say when dinner was being prepared. When we found it necessary to remove the food from the stove, she would still be talking when we returned, oblivious to the fact that we had been away from the telephone.

Yet words are one of life's most precious gifts: our structure for thinking, our bridges of love, our means of sharing life. "Your words have kept men on their feet" (Job 4:4, Moffatt), observed Eliphaz long ago, and he was equally aware of words that would make men wish to die. We live in a world of words, and how easily we become inundated with them. How we long for words of love, hope, truth, understanding, and joy: "A word fitly spoken" (Prov. 25:11) in time and eternity.

All of us understand the meaning of "compulsive talking," the flow of language not for the purpose of communicating but motivated by anxiety, fear, the desire for attention, insecurity, hunger, approval, or inner disturbance. Perhaps, at some time, all of us have been guilty. How do we stop? We isolate the cause within ourselves. Why do I desire attention? Why do I hunger for approval? Why am I anxious and afraid? There is strength in confronting one's fears. When we meet them head-on, they seem less intimidating. We discover we don't have to be victimized by them. Then we turn to the task of learning to love ourselves. This can be more difficult than confronting our fears.

For many, putting themselves down has become so ingrained that eradicating the pattern of thinking, the manner of feeling entailed in self-despising can be awesome. Perhaps self-pity has become a cover for our reluctance to become involved. But God loves us and we can learn to love ourselves. As the apostle Paul wrote young Timothy long ago: "God hath not given us the spirit of fear; but of power, and of love, and of a sound mind" (2 Tim. 1:7).

Knowing you're loved is the first step in overcoming compulsive behavior.

Do You Want to be Free?

1. *Reject complaint; choose the opposite, gratitude.*
2. *Write down your strong points and be thankful for them.*
3. *Let your positive acts dominate your negative feelings.*
4. *Major on life's joys, pleasures, satisfactions.*

12 You and the Green-eyed Monster
Jealousy

"Yet he was jealous, though he did not show it.
For jealousy dislikes the world to know it."
—Byron

"I'm the happiest woman in the world!" the young woman exclaimed. "Have you married the man you love?" asked her friend. "Oh no, I've married the man seven other women love!" It should be impossible but in our competitive way of living, who can say? Jealousy, the highly prevalent and highly denied emotion, causes anxiety, pain, and broken relationships. While not attractive and, easily detected in others, jealousy is rarely confessed. Francis Xavier once admitted in all his years as a priest, he had never heard a confession of jealousy. As a pastor I have heard only one.

He was an eleven-year-old, a bright, clean, and honest youngster, not yet sophisticated enough to put on the mask of pretense. For many months he had been carefully considering the matter of Christian discipleship; he had attended instruction classes, come publicly before the church, and made a witness to his faith and requested baptism. Now a ten-year-old brother was trying to upstage

111

him. "I'm jealous," he confessed with disarming candor and an honest heart, then we had prayed for forgiveness, and his sense of release was immediate and complete. Incidentally, since that morning I often baptize brothers separately, for the beginning of the Christian pilgrimage should be special and joyful.

Do you have trouble with "the embarrassing emotion"? Interestingly, people are willing to confess anger, depression, fear, even greed, but never jealousy. We disavow it, call it by other names, and try to make it respectable. We've done it so long we're not even aware of what we do. Yet jealousy is universal—we live in a competitive world, grow up in homes where we are compared to others, and we are constantly pressed to succeed.

William Shakespeare called jealousy that "green-eyed monster," but we give the emotion better names, and we give ourselves away by our critical tongues and our deprecating looks, tones, and attitudes. I become expert in describing the faults of the minister who is called to the pulpit I secretly desired. I even develop skills in psychoanalyzing his improper motives and unethical maneuvers in securing such a choice assignment, and in the process I become very ethical about myself. "Homely women question the morals of beautiful women," the cynic says, "and the poor always doubt the ethics of the rich." Jealousy can destroy rationality and ruin friendship, even friendships in marriage.

Perhaps you saw that poignant movie, *Amadeus,* the life of Wolfgang Amadeus Mozart, the dazzling musical genius who lived such a tragic and brief life. The whole theme of the movie (which, incidentally, may be overdone) is built around Salieri, Mozart's friend and fellow artist, who was overwhelmed with jealousy when he discovered that a mere youth possessed gifts which he would never have. He understood good music, loved it, and had given his life to it, but he realized he would never be as great a teacher, pianist, composer, or gifted an artist as Mozart. Ironically, Salieri was plagued with the talent to recognize great art in others, but he did not have the gift to produce it himself. His jealousy filled him with pain, anger, rage, and self-doubt. Human gifts are so varied and sometimes seem so irrational that jealousy seems to arise unbidden.

Jealousy has been defined as "an act of careful guarding, resentfully suspicious of a rival or rival's influence . . . requiring exclusive loyalty." Envy and jealousy are not the same, but often they are interrelated. Envy is a "feeling of discontent and ill will because of another's success or advantage or wealth, a dislike of someone because he or she has something you desire." When I'm envious of you, I want something you have. When I'm jealous of you, I'm fearful you may dispossess me of something I think I have: friendship, affection, esteem, sexual intimacy, standing, and position.

Kathleen H. Bernhard in her book *Jealousy: Its Nature and Treatment* defines jealousy as "Possessiveness or a sense of ownership about a person, event or object in the face of a real or perceived threat."[1] Husbands and wives are jealous of people who might steal the affection of their spouses, intruders who may slip in and destroy their intimacy. Ironically, since love requires freedom, jealousy can stifle the affection it is fearful of losing.

There are many kinds of jealousy: romantic or sexual, sibling, childhood and adolescent, male and female, professional, normal, neurotic, and psychotic. Often jealousy has no basis in fact but exists purely in the imagination. Then again, there may be a real reason or a number of reasons for it. There seems to be a difference in the way males and females perceive it. Males, more often, perceive jealousy as competitiveness between rivals and themselves, a loss of status as well as the loss of a partner; whereas, females find in a rival a threat to the relationship. Females more often respond by drawing away or becoming depressed, whereas males react spontaneously, physically, and combatively. A man may shoot his wife's lover, but such a reaction would be rare among women. Jealousy is the motive in at least 10 percent of all murders in the United States however.

Jealousy abounds in the biblical record. Cain was jealous of his brother Abel and eventually took his life. Apparently, Jacob was jealous of Esau and managed, in the end, to supplant him. Saul was jealous of young David, his popularity, his gifts, his vitality, his youth, and his prowess as a warrior. From the beginning, David's music seemed Saul's only therapy for his madness, but at the same time, David appeared to the king to be a constant threat. The other disciples were jealous of James and John and their ambition for the chief seats in Christ's kingdom. Do you suppose there came a day when Naomi became jealous of Ruth? Or who can forget the raw emotions displayed by the angry brothers of the pampered Joseph before they sold him into slavery. No book is so honest or helpful when it comes to addressing the problems and opportunities of our daily life as the Bible.

There is something about jealousy that makes it elusive and difficult to address in a positive, helpful manner. Part of the problem, many believe, is that so few counselors can admit the problem in their own lives. If I cannot admit to the emotion in my own experience, how can I help you address it? Then there is the problem, not of just handling my own jealousy but that of my partner's. "I've always been loyal to my husband," a frustrated wife explains. "Pray tell me how to convince him of that!" My perception can create my own jealousy.

"I'm jealous by nature," she said, "and afraid others will take me for what I have. I have a fine husband, wonderful children, and good friends. How can I learn to trust God and others?" I wanted to say, "Find a loving community. Become a part of it. Learn to love yourself and give yourself away in loving others. And let God love you!" But it is no easy assignment, for so many have despised themselves so long.

First, I can begin by accepting jealousy as a human emotion, normal under certain circumstances, and find positive, healthy ways of dealing with it. At times, nice people feel jealous. Why not admit, at least to yourself, what those around you already know? "I love my husband because he's so open and honest with me," a counselee said to me once. "He says sometimes, 'You know Honey, you're such a beautiful woman. I get jealous for fear somebody will try to take you away from me.' What he's asking for is a little reassurance, and I'm glad he lets me know when he needs it. Our good marriage is built on our honesty with each other." Honesty and consideration must work both ways. There are many ways we can help each other.

Next, I can examine my behavior and determine how it is serving me. There is antagonistic behavior, isolational behavior, and resolutional behavior. (I can respond with anger. I can try to isolate the cause. I can work to resolve the problem.) What is mine, and how is it serving me? When a problem with jealousy arises, you can get out of the relationship, ignore or tolerate the behavior, try to get your partner to stop, or work on your own jealousy. There are three levels of modification: personal, rational, and situational. Don't just stew. Choose a course of action, select a type of behavior, and decide what modification can be made.

Third, I can be honest about my feelings. There are numerous strategies for overcoming jealousy. I can choose one of them and get busy. But first, I must deal honestly with some basic questions:

- How do I feel when I'm jealous?
- How would I like to feel?
- Why do I feel as I do?
- How do I feel about myself in general?
- What causes me to feel insecure, secure?

Finally, I can set up new models in relationships and act in ways that contribute to healing and health. Learning to express feelings openly and honestly can in itself be therapeutic. In addition, lines of communication must be kept open. There must be clear understandings, careful protection of limits and the establishing of ground rules. You can win the battle and lose the war in the jealousy game.

They had been married for sixty years. Their humor was contagious. He made some comment about the candles costing more than the cake on his last birthday, and she said she was "an AWOTA." When I asked for an explanation, she smiled, "A wonderful old thing considering her age." He agreed. Their love was obvious: sensitive, caring, respect for each other's opinions, and watching each other grow with pleasure. When I complimented their marriage, he grinned and said: "We've had our differences, even jealousies, but we're loyal and persevering. She still tries to reform me, but I love her for it. And sometimes I don't agree, but we act like friends, and we're growing." I thought, *They've found ways to handle the pesky emotions, even jealousy, and to prove the struggle worth the effort.*

Handling the Pesky Emotion

1. *Define problems and concerns.*
2. *Give building trust high priority.*
3. *Be honest about your feelings.*
4. *Face the problem. Find a solution. Close it.*
5. *Enrich and enjoy your relationships.*

13 Bless Our Mortgaged Home
Home Relationships

"Choosing a wife or husband is like buying a phonograph record: you get what you like on one side and take what you get on the other side."

Erma Bombeck, newspaper columnist and down-to-earth philosopher, wrote in one of her columns: "Most women become mothers by accident, some by choice, a few by social pressures and a couple by habit. This year nearly 100,000 women will become mothers of handicapped children." Then she speculated on an angel conversing with God about the choice. She concluded such mothers must have patience and laughter. "But Lord," the angel argued about one of them, "I don't think she even believes in you." "No matter." God replied. "I can fix that."

On May 28, 1987, a little poem appeared in the *Mississippi Baptist Record,* reporting the anguish of a patient in the Baptist hospital (Mary Lillian Whitten) who each evening heard a baby cry.

> Baby crying in the night—
> Who will help to make things right?

Angels see this scene below
Jesus loves you—this I know.

Do the parents ever sigh
When they hear a baby cry?
Do they wonder "Where is he?"
Their flesh and blood—their tiny "we."

Baby crying in the night—
Will the little soul take flight?
Even though the tears still flow—
Jesus loves you—this I know.

Of all relationships, none are so significant, so urgent, and so determinative as home relationships. Here we find our models, discover who we are, become persons in our right. And here not only are our houses mortgaged but sometimes our souls as well. Here all our pretenses are stripped away, and we're revealed for what we are: vindictive, cruel, sadistic, inept, blundering, lazy, indifferent, careless, unconcerned or gentle, loving, kind, helpful, organized, and concerned. If we're to bless our mortgaged house we must determine who we are, see our ways with honest candor, accept with gratitude the love proffered us, and share our love with care and abandon.

Are there troubles in your mortgaged house? As you know, to pay the mortgage, desires must be prioritized, budgets made and met, impulses curbed, and wants controlled. But budgets can be in order, bank sheets in balance, life-styles affluent, and hell can displace love. Love is the glue that makes two people one and multiplies, by division, until there is enough to spare. Is your mortgaged house blessed with love? God intended it to be.

Some years back cartoonist Mural B. "Chick" Young,

creator of the "Blondie" comic strip, died at seventy-two.
Now while I'm not a complete "Bumstead" fan (I don't
enjoy the male, "Dagwood," always ending up the goat),
I do respect anyone who can communicate with 75 million
people. Back in 1970, *Life* magazine did a story about the
history of the "Blondie" strip. You see, Young began the
strip with Blondie as a gold digger trailing rich suitors, one
being Dagwood Bumstead. But during early depression
years, playboys and flappers weren't funny. Then Young
made a switch. On February 13, 1933, he married Blondie
and Dagwood, and, as he put it, "got in the kitchen and
started talking about food and sleep." The strip took off.
Young added money, raising a family, and the problem of
bruised egos. The Bumsteads came to epitomize the problems all of us face in trying to find love in family relationships. In our "mortgaged houses," we expose both our
virtues and vices, our loves and our hates.

What can we do to improve our home relationships?
Let's begin with that beautiful text found in 1 Peter 4:8
about the love that covers a "multitude of sins." *In family
relationship, genuine love can cover a multitude of sins.*
Emil Brunner wrote of love as the "unconditional will to
community," and Francis of Assisi called it "the great
courtesy of God." "There is nothing inexorable about
love," Thomas Carlyle once observed. Love's demands are
searching, stringent, and all-inclusive. The ability to give
and receive may be the deepest and most persistent needs
of human personality. The hunger for love is more endur-
ing than sex, more universal than ambition, and more
lasting than power. All of us want to be loved, and we need
desperately to learn how to love others. We need love most

when we deserve it least. Our most haunting and inspiring moments are when we remember being loved like that.

I'm a grandfather now, and I won't tell you how wonderful that is. Our problem is: we learn so much so late. If I could go back I would be a better father. However, there is comfort in the knowledge that if our children knew we loved them, that love covered a multitude of our mistakes. But they must *know* we love them. Children are improved, made more cooperative, joyful, competent, productive by hearing, feeling, and sensing love. Learn the gestures of love, speak the language of love, show your affections, make your approval visible, and do this when they don't deserve it. Love is not pay for good behavior. While all of us need positive reinforcement, and good parents use it often, love is the climate of grace that nourishes healthy relationships.

- Don't be afraid to love your children and show it.
- Tell them how precious they are, both in your sight and God's.
- Remember love has limits, restraints, disciplines.

But the love that covers a "multitude of sins" begins first between husbands and wives and must be maintained and nourished as the years go by. Couples who do not love each other are ill equipped to love children. Perhaps the best gift we give our children is our visible love for each other. Children feel safe and loved when they sense their parents' love for each other. Why is love so difficult to maintain in modern marriage? The statistics for the past two decades are grim although the divorce rate, which has soared since 1968, seems to have reached a plateau. However the likelihood of divorce for newlyweds is still 50 percent if trends follow those of previous decades. And who can estimate the number of marriages where divorce does not occur but where little love is expressed? Why do so many marriages fail? Legally? Emotionally? Pleasurably?

With some it is unrealistic expectations. Some want to cure their loneliness, and marriage can increase it. Some do not love themselves and imagine the love of someone else will cure their self-loathing. Love can be sought not as an expression of self-esteem or of esteem for another, but rather as a means of raising self-esteem that is painfully low. The quest to find someone who will love me and thereby make me love myself cannot succeed, for that problem can only be solved within. Yet millions attempt it over and over again. There is the problem of poor choices in the beginning, divergent values, changing personalities. "She is not the same girl I married." The comment came as a protest from a forty-two-year-old husband. "Of course not!" I replied. "In the past fifteen years she lost her parents and had a hysterectomy. She's changed, and so have you." Then I added, "Be grateful for her loyalty, and show a little creativity in your love."

Marriages are built on who we are and what we do. What kind of people build the best marriages?

- People who believe in themselves and are excited about life.
- People who esteem themselves and their married partners.
- People who acknowledge and use their gifts.
- People who expect and prepare for life's changes.
- People who have many interests and many friends.
- People who are realistic about marriage expectations.

- People who make commitments and live by them.
- People who have a healthy faith in God.

We bring into marriage who we are: our cantankerous ways and our sunny dispositions, our obsessions and our generosities, our prides and our senses of humor, the children of our past and the parents who still reside in us, the warmth of our love and the bitterness of our hate, our winsome ways and our irritating foibles. In bygone days of romance, we believed in Santa Claus, magic, and fairy tales, so, imagine our assets will multiply and our deficits vanish. I have a counselor friend who contends all of us bring five things to our weddings: a steamer trunk of experiences and memories; a book of family rules; a backpack of anger, resentment, and hatred; a duffel bag of guilt, dirty linen, and regrets; and a flight bag of hopes and dreams. Sometimes years are required for unloading our emotional baggage, and much marital conflict finds its source here. However, we also bring into marriage what we do, and love is something we do.

If love is the glue of your marriage, what difference will that glue make in your domestic behavior. How will you treat each other? How do you spell it out?

1. *You treat each other with common courtesy.*

My wife contends I say things to her I wouldn't dare say to the deacons or church members, and, of course, she tells the truth. Why is it we can be models of consideration in the office and holy terrors at home? Why do we manage to be civil, polite, and considerate with people with whom we do business and so often explode with those whom we love? Does familiarity breed contempt? Is it our need to let down when we get home? Do those who know us best, who love and care for us most, become victims of our bottled-up emotions which cannot be ventilated during the day? I'm not certain, but this I know: if we love people, we must treat them with common courtesy. Unless we do, our love can turn to hate, and at best in time, it will dissipate away.

2. *You express your affections.*
If love is something you do, then it does not really exist until it is made tangible. Without language we cannot think, and without words love is a nebulous emotion at best. Why is love so often unexpressed? Parental training? Inability to love ourselves? Fear of rejection? A sense of embarrassment? Whatever the reason, until love is expressed, talked out, acted out, and felt out—it is not love at all.

3. *You are patient with each other.*
In his magnificent hymn of love, the apostle Paul wrote: "Love is very patient, very kind" (1 Cor. 13:4, Moffatt). Perhaps this is where love begins. Do you remember your parents' love with warmth and gratitude? If you do, very likely their love was expressed to you as a child with great patience. But patience is not a natural virtue: it is a learned one. If I love you, I will be patient with you.

4. *You spend time with each other.*
There are 168 hours in a week, 10,080 minutes. How much time do you suppose the average married couple spend talking to each other? No, not twenty hours or ten, or even thirty minutes. The average is seventeen minutes, and then they wonder why they grow apart. Love has and shows genuine interest in other people, and love begins in listening.

5. *You are loyal and faithful.*
The best marriages have freedom built into them, and both partners have many friends, but I am convinced that the biblical injunction against adultery was given—not to frustrate us—but to protect us. Sexuality is one of God's joyful gifts and is to be expressed with exuberance and thanksgiving, but sex like all emotions must be disciplined and controlled. Perhaps, at some time, every married person is attracted to someone else, but wise spouses have discovered that to work at improving themselves and the marriage of which they are a part is both more satisfying and more rewarding.

6. *You let God's love make your love divine.*
Perhaps we start with romance and dreams, moonlight and roses but soon enough—sometimes too soon—we come to conflict and reality, dirty dishes and diapers, and our romance demands reality, or it disappears. But as we address "our common clay," we begin to see the true image of God within us, and the kind of love that gives life meaning and purpose. We struggle together, work together, pray together, and sometimes suffer together; but in the process, we discovery His love which begins to make our love divine—slowly at first, sometimes imperceptibly, but in the end like a benediction. Tolstoy's story title said it well: "Where love is, there is God also."

You Want Your Mortgaged Home Less Mortgaged:

1. *Spend your money and affection for what you really want.*
2. *Make conflict your friend.*
3. *Take pride in each other's growth.*
4. *Forget reforming; love is more fun.*

14   Kids, Kids, Kids!
From a Parent's Perspective

"He who fights the future has a dangerous enemy."
—Soren Kierkegaard

"Parents get the children they deserve." Often I've wondered who originated that proverb, or indeed, if it is a proverb. Perhaps some adult, with no children, who knew all the answers about rearing them said it. You see, I'm not sure I believe the proverb. Perhaps the lousy parents get the children they deserve; but the good parents, not always. By the time children discover their parents were really good, the parents are dead.

Parenting is an humbling experience, a revealing and searching one. Our children tell us so many things about ourselves, and they have endless ways of forcing us to retract our boastful predictions. If you must be the popular hero, then don't have kids. Parental love must be stronger than that. Children not only bless us, they teach us, open our minds and hearts, and compel us to learn flexibility and grace.

Benjamin Franklin is reported to have written an extensive dissertation on child-rearing. Then, one was born in his home, and he went through his learned composition and marked out several sentences. Some time later, a second child was born, and he again reviewed his paper, and marked out all but the final paragraph. Later when the third child came, Franklin marked out that final paragraph and wrote, "Do the best you can under the circumstances."

Thomas Kepler, the eminent astronomer, having failed in his first marriage, resolved to put his second one on a sound scientific basis. He listed all the women he considered eligible, then on one side he tabulated their virtues and on the other, their vices. He graded each item and tabulated the results by exact mathematical calculations. But the second marriage turned out worse than the first one. Perhaps Kepler failed to factor in his own vices. Regardless, the baffled man announced his problem was insoluble. What he missed was the human factor and the laws of love.

I read once about a father who became impatient with his twenty-one-year-old son's progress and wrote to urge him on. The journalist son, annoyed with his ambitious father, wrote back, admitting his progress had not been spectacular, but he knew exactly where he was going. With tongue-in-cheek, the son wrote that at thirty he expected to be a great newspaper reporter, at forty a great city editor, at fifty a great short-story writer, at sixty a great novelist, at seventy a great-grandfather, at eighty a great admirer of pretty women, and at ninety a great loss to the community. He felt his father had asked for it, and he confessed that excluding the word *great* he had kept pretty much on schedule.

Parents and kids need to start early being human beings. What do I mean by that? As a parent:

- You don't pretend to know all the answers.
- You set up reasonable boundaries and stick to them, and you admit, even to your kids, that you make mistakes.
- You learn to be honest about your feelings and encourage your kids to be.
- You let your kids know your love is unconditional.

As a kid:

- You accept your parents, flaws and all, and remember that without them you wouldn't be here.
- Parents make mistakes, and so do you. They'll answer for their mistakes, and you'll answer for yours.
- Don't spend your life resenting *their* mistakes; it's healthier to resent your own.
- They deserve your thanks.
- Be glad you're an improvement.

A father sat absorbed in his evening paper. His five-year-old interrupted him, "Daddy, do you love God?" "Why, yes, of course!" "But Daddy, have you ever seen God?" "No," the father said impatiently, "no one ever has." "Daddy, how can you love Him if you've not seen him?" Irritated, the father replied, "Oh, be quiet. Don't you see I'm trying to read the paper!" The child was quiet for a few minutes, then putting his hand on his daddy's knee, he said, "But, Daddy, I do want to know!"

Fathers deal with such matters whether they discuss them or not. Our children know how we feel, what we value, who we worship, and nearly always make those values their own. What makes a Christian family?

1. The place it gives to Jesus Christ. Nothing affects a home so much as its choice of priorities.
2. The use it makes of its material resources. Money talks, and money reveals.
3. The quality of its circle of friends. One cannot be a Christian alone.
4. The degree of love it shows. Love unexpressed is not love, only an abstraction.

Although my parents have been gone for some time, I often think of them and rejoice in their love. Did they ever despair of me in my childhood? Perhaps. Sometimes I make lists of happy memories from my childhood: Christmas fun, Daddy's approval, springtime, Sunday dinner, good sleep, books, dreams, ice tea with a lot of ice, homemade ice cream, knowing sexual feelings were not bad, picnics, being special, and Christmas worship. And then I remember the joys of our own children. I think there are some very important facts we parents need to remember:

1. Every parent feels like a failure at some time.
2. If our kids know we love them, they can survive many difficulties.
3. Love is mostly patience.
4. God loved them before we did.
5. Faith is best taught by example.
6. The best gift is yourself.
7. Discipline is training in self-control.
8. It is folly to squander authority.
9. Make meals joyful.
10. All parents begin wanting to do the impossible— safeguard their lives forever from all pain, all danger,

and all struggle. (To do so would create zombies). It is neither wise nor possible.

11. A parent's business is to work himself out of a job.
12. Sometimes all we can do is watch and pray.

There is a fascinating story from the life of Phillips Brooks, the New England preacher. Like most young people who grow up in homes of strong religious faith, there came a day when Brooks declared his religious independence from his parents. Home from university, he came into the kitchen one day and announced with great finality to his mother: "I don't believe in God." Unperturbed, his mother continued to mix her pie crust. Somewhat disturbed by his failure to get a rise, young Brooks repeated, "Mother, I've decided that I cannot believe in God." Smiling, his mother replied: "Very well, Phil, your mother does." That was all. That was enough. She had laid the foundation well.

How to Enjoy Your Kids

1. *Don't expect perfection; remember they're kids.*
2. *Let them know you love them, every day.*
3. *Be glad you've survived.*
4. *Let God share the responsibility.*

15 Parents, Parents, Parents!
From a Kid's Perspective

"They're driving me crazy."

—A teenager

These two chapters are written for parents—the previous chapter from the perspective of the parent and this one from the perspective of the child. I'd be pleased if a child were to read both, but I don't expect that to happen. Putting oneself in someone else's place is both rare and different. Perhaps the child cannot do it. (No child can love a parent like a parent loves a child until the child becomes a parent). Few parents do. Although I once was a child, how rarely I see my child through a child's eyes. Memory has a way of erasing the embarassing, unpleasant, and humiliating. Too often, childhood includes such experiences. However, to be a good parent, to show love and even affection, we must try to put ourselves in the places of our children, understand how they feel and think and perceive.

"They're driving me crazy!" The comment came from an anguished teenager. I wanted to respond, "You may be driving them crazy too," but I refrained, thinking what my young friend needed most at the moment was a listening ear and an understanding heart. Feelings need to be expressed and heard.

How long has it been since you made an effort to put yourself in your child's place? I have a friend who, when he sees a child being roughly treated, responds, "But he's just a little fellow." He smiles and says, "That is better than calling the 'big bully' what he really is." Think about it. The child is small; you're large. He's helpless; you have all the power. He's dependent; you're autonomous. He has opinions, but people rarely ask him for them or even listen when he tries to tell them. He's trying to find ways to see himself as separate, worthwhile, useful, and you're always telling him what to do. Sometimes he feels, when it comes to him, the only words you know are "Don't," "Stop," "No." You pushed him out of his nest before he wanted to go, had another baby while he thought he had all your love, and now all you do is correct him. You can understand his explosion that day when he cried out, "Mommy, I'll shoot you dead!" Did you censor and shame him, or respond, "I know how you feel"?

> My mom says I'm her sugar plum.
> My mom says I'm her lamb.
> My mom says I'm completely perfect,
> Just the way I am.
> My mom says I'm a super-special wonderful terrific
>   little guy.
> My mom just had another baby.
> Why?[1]

Little wonder kids sometimes ask, "When do we take the new baby back to the hospital?" But with love, affection, understanding, patience, and parental care, they learn there is enough love for all. But they deserve our patience and understanding.

Perhaps an even greater problem for us parents is seeing our children as separate individuals. They begin as part of us, but the whole purpose of parenthood is to work ourselves out of a job. The end of parenting is healthy, happy, mature men and women who can stand on their own feet and live productive lives. Yet how often as parents we see them as extensions of ourselves, expect them to make us look good, to be grateful for the opportunities we have given them, and to be improvements on us. Letting our children go is also letting go of our expectations for them. This entails respecting their right to choose the shape of their own lives. You see, when we have children, a new dream is born in the world—the dream of keeping them safe from every harm. Although noble in origin, it is neither always possible or always wise. To avoid all pain is to avoid growth, understanding, and strength. We have to let go of so much of what we had hoped we could do for them. Just as they must separate from us, so we must separate from them. We have to learn that however much of our lives we devote to them, there is a world within them and outside of them we do not control.[2]

Do you ever wonder how many frustrated children there are? When you take into account the broken homes, the rate of divorce, the drug addiction, the violence of our society, the narcotizing effect of television, teenage pregnancies, and the confused morality of our age—you're amazed at how many healthy kids there are. Human beings are amazingly resourceful for survival, and they overcome many mistakes in childhood. Yet how we treat our children matters enormously. When a million American

youth run away from home every year, something needs
to be done.

"They're driving me crazy!" Sometimes I hear that cry
of desperation in the night. How do we drive our children
to despair?

1. *By never hearing what they say.*
True listening is complicated and difficult work, and perhaps most of us don't listen because we are not that concerned, and we don't want to work that hard. There is ear
listening, eye listening, head listening, and listening that
hears feelings and heartaches. To listen is to say, "I care
for you. You are important to me. I want to understand
how you think and feel and dream and hope." To listen
is to say, in perhaps the most convincing way, "I love you
and want the best for you." Our children deserve attention.

2. *By treating them like children and expecting them to*
   act like adults.
In the United States we have the "longest adolescence" in
the world. In Colonial days, soon after puberty, young
people entered careers and were married. Today, with
years of extended education, there is a kind of adolescence
that can extend to thirty or beyond. The media and its
obsession with sex, violence, and crime is robbing children
of their childhood, and youth are subjected to the inflam-
ing of the most powerful human drives. We have no
choice, but both in teaching and discipling to help our
children take on adult roles.

3. *By refusing to give of ourselves to them.*
Why do we imagine our children prefer gifts to us? Is it
because we find *things* easier to give them than ourselves?

A wonderful friend and popular clergyman, who had too many away-from-home speaking engagements, found his six-year-old daughter painfully disappointed in his upcoming absence. He asked her to help him prepare his address: *"Being a Good Father."* Her list was poignantly revealing: A good daddy knows how to make a fire, catch a butterfly, fly a kite, catch a fish, play a game, and sing a song."[3]

4. *By making our love conditional.*
Conditional love isn't love at all. To love is to accept, affirm, understand, believe in, and bring out the best in other people. To make demands, to state conditions, to threaten, and to lay on guilt is to increase fear not confidence. "There is no fear in love; but perfect love casteth out fear: . . . He that feareth is not made perfect in love" (1 John 4:18). Let them know they belong to you and you to them, and nothing can ever change that. Your love will release their love and multiply it.

5. *By our inability to admit our faults.*
"I shall never forget that night when my daddy admitted he was wrong and asked me to forgive him. He took me in his arms, and sobbing, said he loved me. Somehow that night I knew I could be forgiven too." The confession had come fifty years after a father's death and had opened tide gates of comfort and joy.

6. *By not caring enough to say no.*
Love is not synonymous with being indifferent, indulgent, or free and easy. If I love you I want you to be strong, self-controlled, productive, useful, and adult. Perhaps the first step in becoming a person in our own right is to discover our limitations, the perimeters of our being. I am not adult until the conscience others exercised for me

becomes internalized within me. People who love us help
us set limits that are reasonable and for our good.

7. *By being unwilling to set them free.*
Love involves both saying no and yes, and one of the
trickiest parts of parenthood is knowing when to say no
and when to say yes. Without restraint, young children
destroy themselves, but if they're to grow and mature,
they must become gradually equipped to make decisions
for themselves. Historians tell us that Edward VII, the son
and successor of Queen Victoria, was so dominated by his
mother that even at the age of fifty, if late for a court
dinner, he would hide behind a pillar in terror and not
dare come to sit at the table. Even kings can be crippled
by domineering parents.

8. *By being inconsistent about our own faith.*
Love makes us vulnerable, but love also makes us visible.
It strips us bare and exposes our true values for all to see.
Nobody knows what we really worship like our kids. If we
love God, they know we do by the tone of our voices, the
use we make of our resources, and the way we spend our
time. I could tell by the tone in my mother's voice how she
felt about the Bible, and my grandmother never gave me
a lecture on the importance of the church, but everything
about her proved it. Nowhere is honesty so important,
nowhere is candor so healthy, nowhere is openness so
necessary with our children as in matters of faith. If ours
is real, there is a deposit within them which time does not
erase. Isn't that what Proverbs 22:6 means? "Train up a
child in the way he should go: and when he is old, he will
not depart from it."

To be good parents, to help our children grow, and to
let love come alive in our relationships we need a model

or perhaps many models both in words and in people. We need to ask ourselves what made Amram and Jochebed (the parents of Moses), Zacharias and Elizabeth (the parents of John the Baptist), and Joseph and Mary (the parents of Jesus) good parents? What did they do right? What can they teach us?

We also need to investigate the apostle Paul's principle, stated in Ephesians 6:1-4, if we wish to help our children make it through the day and make it through life. The principle, "Submitting [ourselves] one to another in the fear of God" (Eph. 5:21), is radical and new but voluntary and grounded in love. We choose to submit ourselves to each other. That submission involves children obeying their parents in keeping with God's ancient laws of human happiness and parents not provoking their "children to wrath" but rearing them "in the nurture and admonition of the Lord." The parent's authority—while God given—is temporary and subject to the God who gave it.

In the context of that kind of love, we do not drive each other crazy; we make each other glad.

How to Vent the Steam

1. *Hear what they say.*
2. *Limit your rules and stick to them.*
3. *Let them know you love them.*
4. *Be proud of their growth.*
5. *And finally, let them loose.*

16 Check the Fusebox
Anger

"Whom the gods would destroy, they first make mad."
—A Proverb

"Anger's my meat," wrote William Shakespeare long ago, "I sup upon myself." But it was Horace, the Latin poet, who called it "momentary madness."

Of all the emotions, anger is the most primitive, the most obvious, the most pleasant, and the most perilous. This least-civilized human attribute springs from one of the oldest and deepest parts of the brain. This small clump of cells lies dwarfed under the large mass called the cerebrum, the "grey matter" that enables us to reason, be gentle and kind, and do heroic things. We might dismiss this tiny clump of cells as insignificant were it not for the devastating destruction anger has caused in the world. How often this is the emotion behind violence, murder, and armed conflict. Every penitentiary is filled with dozens of model prisoners who, in some fit of anger, took someone's life. Yes, anger is the most primitive and obvious of emotions. We see it, sense it, feel it, even enjoy it, and then regret it—sometimes forever.

We sometimes enjoy it. Do you agree? There can be a

bizarre kind of pleasure to the one who is angered. When you feel mistreated, affronted, injured, anger, if unchecked, can drive you to retaliate. Feeling your adversary deserves it, there is an irrational kind of satisfaction in giving him what he deserves. Yet nothing is so perilous both for the victim and the perpetuator. What, in a moment seemed exhilarating, can become the regrets of a lifetime.

There are students of human behavior who contend we come into the world angry because of the discomfort of birth. "The human child begins his life in anger," once observed Karl Menninger. The small child soon suffers other frustrations. Two-year-olds have been called "the angriest people in the world." Since they cannot defend themselves, who knows?

Many things feed anger. When events frustrate, disappoint, and abuse us, when we are annoyed at ourselves or others, we tend to become angry. Sometimes the cause is infringement: someone violating our territory. Sometimes it is frustration, and perhaps more often, a perception of injustice. Woolfolk and Richardson in *Stress, Sanity and Survival* suggest anger-producing factors. Some become angry because *they have too much on the line.* They suffer from overidentification with countries, classes, causes, parties, and on and on. They feel they must defend the army, the navy, the air force, capitalism, professional football, and our American way of life. Indeed, if their friends have any independent opinions on anything, the defenders tend to react with hostility. A second factor is *approaching life competitively rather than cooperatively.* There's an example in almost every office. What causes it? Is it a product of our spectator sports' syndrome obsessed with

winning rather than enjoying playing the game? Ironically, many lawyers, doctors, and ministers see other professional men and women not as colleagues but as
competitors, not as allies but as rivals, not as friends but
as antagonists. They live competitively, not cooperatively,
and constantly raise the anxiety level. Then there is *the
problem of moralistic thinking,* getting angry when others
violate our rules of conduct. When we think in terms of
what others should and should not do, we open ourselves
to irritation. Often anger is fed when we *attribute to others
motives for their actions.* Husbands and wives are often
guilty at this point, assuming they understand inner feelings when they have made no effort to do so. Again anger
can come from a *low tolerance for discomfort.* Oversen-
sitivity guarantees frequent anger.

We lose our tempers for a variety of reasons, recognized
and unrecognized. Jean-Paul Sartres thought anger an
expression of defeat. Anger can come from humiliation, a
sense of helplessness, exhaustion, or even hunger. Often
anger arises from unresolved childhood trauma. The expressions of anger are equally varied, ranging all the way
from pugnacity to withdrawal. "Bottled anger" may be
the deadliest anger of all. Depression can be caused by
inverted anger.

Anger is less destructive and more easily controlled
when we understand its causes, but the primary question
is how are we to respond to this difficult emotion.

How do you deal with your anger? What were you
taught as a child? (1) Be strong. (2) Be perfect. (3) Never
show your temper. (4) Work hard. (5) Be careful. (6)
Hurry up. (7) Please me. To deny feelings is not to conquer them but to guarantee they will cause future trouble.

Anger is a normal, natural human emotion, and to deny its existence, refuse to admit it, or try to conceal it makes it more difficult to handle. People wear dozens of masks to conceal their anger: withdrawal, silence, indifference, feigned cordiality, hyperactivity, and strained relationships. When things go wrong at the office, we take it out on our families; when things go wrong at home, we take it out on our employees. Sometimes we project it on other people, and sometimes we turn it in upon ourselves.

Our primary concern is: How do we deal with our anger in a healthy, helpful manner? How do we avoid the pain and remorse it can bring? How do we make it through that angry day and go to sleep at night?

First, we admit that experiencing the emotion of anger is not a sin. We are explicitly commanded by the Bible, "Be ye angry, and sin not: let not the sun go down upon your wrath" (Eph. 4:26). The capacity for anger is necessary for survival, development, growth, and change. Any healthy, normal human being who is alive and sensitive will feel it periodically. Indeed there may be times when not to feel it would be sin. To not feel it could imply callousness, insensitivity, or obstinate blindness in the presence of human need. Jesus became angry because of the exploitation of human beings. There seems to be no indication Jesus ever showed anger because someone affronted him. What He cautioned about was "Anyone who nurses anger against his brother" (NEB) (Matt. 5:21-22). Like Proverbs, Jesus points out that anger nursed and cultivated is a dangerous thing. Let us begin with the understanding that anger is a natural and even healthy human emotion which can energize us for action.

Second, we remember either to continually repress or to

allow unbridled expressions of anger can be devastating.
Repressed anger surfaces in myriads of unpleasant and
damaging ways. We must learn to admit our anger, get it
out, and learn to express it in ways that neither damage
others or ourselves. We must learn how anger can be
beneficial. Many feel intimacy is strengthened when anger
is expressed openly and constructively, when fighting is
done fairly and redemptively. Anger can serve as a danger
signal, a warning especially about breakdown in relationships. Anger can push toward independence. Perhaps
without anger most of us would never get started on the
road to individual freedom. Anger can help uncover guilt
and shame and give impetus and power to our struggle
against injustice and oppression.

*Then after recognizing what causes our anger, we can
isolate the things that trigger it, and either avoid them or
learn to keep them in perspective.* In this way we both
lessen our vulnerability and keep our priorities in better
order. We develop safe outlets, enhance emotional maturity, and find life more satisfying and joyful. When we're
happy, we find ourselves becoming angry far less often.

We can focus our anger by staying in touch with our
feelings so we are not caught off guard. We learn to voice
anger without creating chaos and when necessary put it in
a safe place until we can handle it redemptively. If we
cannot make it our friend, we can at least make it our
teacher.

*Finally, since anger is energy and must go somewhere, we
can learn to spend it wisely and keep it under control.*
Anger is not always the opposite of love; sometimes it is
its clearest expression. Bishop Channing wrote: "Or-
dinarily, I weigh 120 pounds; when I'm mad, I weigh a

ton." Anger has been called "one of the sinews of the soul." John Wesley, Abraham Lincoln, and Martin Luther King, Jr., have all been driven by anger caused by injustice. One of the tragedies of our time is our lack of indignation at the tragic injustices all around us. Our society suffers because there are so few Elijahs, Amoses, and John the Baptists. Martin Luther reported that when he was angry both his preaching and praying were improved. Our lack of anger can sometimes be proof of our lovelessness.

Let me give what I call "my four lines":

> Recognize it, admit it, accept it.
> Learn what triggers it.
> Find healthy ways to express it.
> Turn it on causes that matter.

"The washer isn't working, Dear," my wife said. "Have you checked the fuse?" was my response. In the world of household appliances, the fuse is an ingenious safety devise which, when something goes wrong in the circuitry, cuts off the power to keep the appliance from being destroyed.

For the believer, when anger explodes, the love circuit —God's love for us and our love for God—is the fuse, the safeguard for the welfare of the person and the community. Love, a many-splendored thing, expresses itself in myriads of ways. Check the fuse!

How to Handle Anger

1. *Admit it even if you feel uncomfortable.*
2. *Get control of yourself. Inhale deeply, think of something pleasant, and work it out if you can.*

3. *If possible, tell the person you're angry at what you resent, and that you want to learn.*
4. *Find ways to relieve the daily tension.*
5. *Keep trying to be honest and open about your feelings.*

17 When Your Getup Has Gone
Motivation

"When we accept ourselves as we are, then we can change."

—Carl Rogers

Millions of people feel that way every morning, but they get up anyway for the widest variety of reasons. Some though force of habit, some to support a family, some because they find their work stimulating or compelling, and some because they don't know what else to do. Some get up because they want to make money, satisfy an ambition, get a promotion, be with people, make a name for themselves, or prove something. Some hate their work but get up anyway. Nothing is more important than *knowing why* we do what we do. The motives back of our deeds often reveal the kind of persons we are.

Motivation has been called the forces within us which cause the arousal, direction, and persistence of behavior. Human beings have always been fascinated, and perplexed by these forces that cause us to act as we do. The ancients saw the will as the essential source behind human deeds and the will as determined by what intelligence perceives to be reasonable and good. They saw human beings as free because we are rational, because we are not driven into action by an external cause without our consent and because we can choose between the means of realizing good or the purpose which our reason conceives. Plato and Aristotle thought knowledge the determinant of behavior. But they did not believe knowledge alone in and of itself sufficient to determine behavior. Will was to them even more important. Thomas Aquinas saw animal behavior as motivated by instincts but human behavior by rational insights.

In our day, motivation has been examined from almost endless perspectives: Freud with his systems of tension reduction stemming from basic instinctual sources such as hunger, thirst, and sex; others have emphasized survival motivation relating to evolutionary development, or aggression as a consequence of frustration, and motivation as a reflection of rigid value systems, all the way to Maslow's theories of self-actualization, growth, and development. Motivational forces are complex and varied. We know how often imagination overpowers reason, how astute we are at rationalization, how clever in projecting on others our own faults, and how we deceive others and ourselves.

The small boy was trying to reach the doorbell. An elderly lady, passing by, stopped and lifted him up, so he could ring the bell. He rang for several minutes, and then the lady asked, "Now what do we do next?" "Run like crazy!" exclaimed the boy. She had misread his motives. A man understands what motivates his wife, and she understands what motivates him, but he's at a loss when it comes to understanding what motivates himself. Actually nothing is more complex, puzzling, and enigmatic than human motivation. The Caesars had their "bread and circuses," God-fearing people in the Middle Ages brought young children to watch the hanging of a prisoner or the burning of a "witch," and we have an addiction to a kind of Sunday afternoon mayhem called professional football. What motivates us to be drawn for an exhibition of someone else's pain?

When it comes to dealing with motivation, inner healing begins with objectivity and honesty. But motivational honesty can be painful. "How can I overcome my habit of exaggeration?" D. L. Moody was asked by a prominent businessman. "Why don't you begin by facing the fact that what you call 'exaggeration' in yourself you call 'lying' in other people?" Moody answered.

William James pointed out that "inconsistent behavior" often finds its source in "the unconscious, the part of us that forgets nothing and lies beneath the surface." For example, the master of ceremonies at a large banquet is actually revealing, unintentionally, what his "subconscious" really thinks when he says, "Before our distinguished guest commences his speech, I have something important to say." Or the eight-year-old daughter, who, after looking over the visitor intently, says, "Oh, my, but you aren't plain!" Embarrassed, the mother says to her child, "Whatever do you mean? Apologize at once!" "I only meant it for a joke," explains the child. Her mother, hoping to smooth things over, says, "It would have been a much better joke if you had said, 'How pretty you are!'"

When it comes to motives we have dozens of ways of deceiving ourselves like the woman who goes in for community service "to help the unfortunate" when what she really wants is social approval. We give for many reasons:

of guilt, to impress others, and to help the needy. The other day I read a devastating sentence: "It was written all over him: My renunciation is greater than yours." Or like the teacher who had killed so many Sunday School classes that everything about him said, "You're so fortunate to have the privilege of hearing me teach."

Honesty about motives is a secret of health and happiness. Do you catch yourself projecting your faults on your friends? Do you excuse in yourself what you condemn in others? One way to begin checking on your motives is to be at least as generous with other people's foibles as you are with your own. A sense of humor will help. When a father boasted to his son, "Yes, Son, I'm a self-made man," the boy replied, "Gee, Dad, that's what I like about you; you take the blame for everything." How can God's cleansing and healing power begin to work in us unless we bring ourselves to confront what really motivates us?

We must accept our mixed motivation and be honest and forthright with ourselves. When our motives are honest and healthy, we can be glad and affirm them. When they're not, we can try to understand what causes them and plan ways to redirect them. We can subject our motives to the mind of Christ but at the same time be aware of our humanity. All motives need not be noble, some can and should be merely natural and healthy. Human beings eat when they're hungry, sleep when they're tired, laugh when they're amused, weep when they're sad, crave attention, long for intimacy (both sexual and otherwise), and feel anger. These are not evil in themselves but natural, normal, and a part of the energy of life. We must accept them, learn to control them, and live with them creatively and joyfully. Healthy motivation has to do with being healthy human beings. Be noble sometimes, but just live sometimes. Life's made up of both.

But you protest that your problem is not unhealthy motivation: it is no motivation at all. You've lost your zest for life, your ambition is depleted, your has enthusiasm faded, and you would prefer not to get up in the morning. What can you do?

- *Find out why your joy is gone.* Are you depressed, fed up, or bored? Perhaps you resent unfair treatment, repeated slights, and lack of appreciation from your associates. Have you had too much criticism and put yourself under too much pressure? Is the problem in you or in others?
- *Take a break. Find a temporary diversion.* Get away for a period. (But don't make major decisions while you are down.)
- *If you're ill, see a doctor.*
- *Every day do something for pure enjoyment, if only for ten minutes.* This does not include feeling sorry for yourself. If you find joy in this you are caught in the trap of self-pity, and you need professional help.
- *Reevaluate your gifts with someone else's help.*
- *Admit what you don't like.* Honest hatred is healthier than pretended friendship. As a Christian, you are not commanded to like everybody, just act with *agape* toward them. Anger confronted, ventilated, and redirected can be a powerful force for healing and health.
- *Reward yourself more often.* You deserve praise as well as blame.

- *Share your fun if you have any, and if not, remember it will return.*
- *Unless your doctor tells you to stay in bed, get up in the morning.* Keep moving. Activity will probably improve your feelings. You'll be glad you did!

I've been watching my grandchildren. "If I had known how much fun grandchildren are, I would have had them first," a friend of mine says. What motivates a young child to learn to crawl, to stand erect, to walk, to talk, and to communicate? Talk about miracles! In the course of a few months, children master some of the most complicated and difficult skills on earth. How do they do it? Is it something God put within them, something programmed in their genes? Or is it the newness, the excitement, and the wonder of participating with other human beings? I think it is the latter. Did you ever listen to a child laugh after taking his first step? Or see the light in his eyes when he discovers he has communicated with someone else?

It is the good use of life, its intrinsic joy that fills us with wonder, and motivates us to fruitful living. "The joy of the Lord" is indeed our strength and should become our song.

To Help You Get Up in the Morning

1. *Think of those you love.*
2. *Count your blessings.*
3. *Be glad you're alive.*
4. *Name one thing you can do.*
5. *Remember Jesus Christ.*

18   Breaking the Dishes Won't Help
Frustration

"The mind is its own place, and in itself can make a heaven of hell, a hell of heaven."

—John Milton

Frustrations come in many guises, losses that arise from within us and from without, real or imagined, disappointments, defeats, events we can alter and things immutable, and frequently from both. Does this line from an old song ever describe your feelings: "I'm a troubled man singing a troubled song"?

Marian Anderson, the great contralto, made her debut in New York's Town Hall too early in her career. Prepared neither in experience nor training, she was devastated by the critics' reviews and returned to Philadelphia crushed. Her church and friends had raised the money for her debut, and she could barely face them. Her always-supportive mother refused to give up and stood beside her, advising, "Marian, grace must come before greatness. Why don't you think about this failure a *little* and pray about it a *lot?*"[1] Marian did just that—one way among many to deal with frustration.

Frustration has been termed "failure to accomplish

something meaningful to you," and Marian Anderson's failure was painfully frustrating. It might have ended Miss Anderson's career had she and those she loved succumbed to temporary defeat.

How did Miss Anderson cope? Was it other frustrations already confronted, the love and devotion of those who surrounded her, her faith in God, and her own ability? Perhaps a combination of these made that night in Town Hall only a stepping-stone toward a brilliant career.

When minor events frustrate us, they should be taken lightly and straightway forgot. Mulled over, they tend to grow. A sense of humor and the ability to laugh at oneself can relieve the pressure. In time, we may take delight in recalling those embarrassing incidents.

Dr. Clovis Chappell, the famous Methodist minister, told of one such happening from his student days at Yale. He and a friend who was a Harvard student traveled home together on holidays. Once as they returned, Chappell purchased his ticket, stuck it in his coat pocket as he spied his friend, and together they boarded the train.

Seeing Chappell's ticket sticking out of his pocket, the Harvard "friend" lifted it from his pocket.

When the conductor started down the aisle, Chappell reached for his ticket and could not find it.

"What will I do?" he asked his friend.

"I guess buy another ticket," his friend responded.

"I don't have enough money!"

"Then the only thing is for you to crawl under the seat until the conductor passes through the car."

Chappell did this. When the conductor stopped at their seat, the Harvard guy handed him two tickets. The conductor asked, "Why two tickets?"

"Oh, I have a Yale friend down there under the seat," the friend explained.

"Why is he down there?" the conductor asked.

"All I know," said the Harvard man, "is that Yale men like to ride that way!"

On hearing that story, a friend said, "That's a cause for murder, not laughter." Nevertheless, it calls for laughter, not tears. No doubt Chappell found a way to even the score with his friend. Think of all the fun he had telling that story in the years to come.

Hypersensitivity produces needless frustration, and accepting our own identity, value, and worth in God's sight makes us relaxed about ourselves and cognizant of everyone's worth and the image of God within.

A legendary Montana cowboy is said to have entered the town saloon on a Saturday night, laid down his money, and said, "Let's drink and be somebody."

But everyone is somebody, no matter how unlovely his or her actions or condition or seeming potential. "Down in the human heart,/Crush'd by the tempter,/Feelings lie buried that grace can restore." That's the way the hymn writer Fanny Crosby put it.

But there are frustrations that relate to our idealism. The more deeply we care, the greater our potential for frustration. Love is, as the Bible declares, the best way of all, but it *may* be the costliest. When Paul wrote in First Corinthians that love is the best way of all, he was not saying that love is the *easiest* way of all. To love in the Christian sense is to become vulnerable, and redemptive love, on whatever level, is sacrificial.

Distinguishing between outside and inside frustration helps us deal with stress. The damage of stress lies more in our response to pressure than in the pressures themselves, and each person brings his or her cluster of past experiences and how they were handled, to the present incident. Powerful and potentially deadly emotions may set off feelings which work havoc inside us.

When I say, "You frustrate me," I may be telling you more about myself than about you. Frustration comes when something very meaningful to one's happiness or success is denied.

Distinguishing between frustration and related emotions, such as anxiety, is helpful. One is frustrated when desires are blocked, ambitions or plans thwarted, and pleasures denied. One is anxious when apprehension dominates. Anxiety is a worried life-style, and its causes are myriad: fear of losing your job or inability to cope with promotion to a more demanding one, whether or not your child is on drugs, your mother has cancer, or your house insurance is adequate. Frustration tends to be episodic, but anxiety tends to breed on itself until it becomes a life-style.

Objectivity is an acute problem in handling frustration. All of us are experts when it comes to someone else, but we are not nearly so objective when our own paths are blocked. Often we ask, "Why do you let that bother you?" We may resent others asking us the same question when we are vexed by an unsolvable problem.

There is an exercise I have found helpful in assessing levels of frustration. I call it "Grading Levels of Frustration." What degree of frustration does the following create in you?

- Being told by a neighbor to "get lost" or where to go.

- Losing a tennis, golf, or handball match.
- An associate publicly embarrasses you.
- You are unable to help a suffering friend.
- Watching a child in pain.
- Witnessing a parent abuse a child.
- Experiencing repeated failure.
- Being the butt of a practical joke.
- Unfairly condemned by someone.
- You are reamed out by the boss.
- Watching a marriage fail.
- Discovering someone has damaged your car.
- Someone exposes one of your worse faults in public.
- Missing what you very much want and receiving something far different.

Your response reveals your emotional stability, your balance, your character, and your maturity. We are revealed both in our pleasures and in our irritations, and healing begins with honesty.

Frustration is fed by many things such as anger, threat, infringement, injustice, slight, challenge, failure, defeat, and embarrassment. Things which cause you anger can cause frustration. Some see frustration as a milder form of the madness called "anger." Perhaps this milder emotion reeks its havoc more slowly, but that is debatable. Is anger more easily ventilated, more universally seen as potentially destructive, and more identifiable?

What can be done about our frustrations? How can we learn to endure them, reduce their emotional fallout, conquer them, and indeed learn from them?

- Accept them as a part of life and learn to take them in stride.

- Let them energize us rather than defeat us. When frustrated, decide what to do about it. Let your irritation motivate you to positive action.
- Laugh when we can about it when we're wrong, and use our energy to plan other strategies.
- Magnify our assets, rejoice in our victories, and give ourselves credit when we deserve it.
- Maybe modify our ambitions.
- See flexibility as an asset and be proud when you can be flexible.
- Resolve not to be unnerved by criticism but to learn from it.
- Seek a positive attitude toward failure as a necessary step to success.
- Stop playing God, and learn to trust His love.

This chapter began with reference to Marian Anderson. A reporter once asked her to name the greatest moment in her life.

She said there had been many, such as the night when Toscanini told her that hers was the first voice of the century or when she sang before the president of the United States and the king and queen of England or that Sunday when she sang to seventy-five thousand people in Washington at the Lincoln Memorial.

It was none of these, she said. Her greatest moment was when she went home and informed her widowed mother that her mother wouldn't have to work any more.[2]

The most remarkable thing about Marian Anderson was not her voice but her character. Character that includes grace is our best cure for frustration.

Ways to Avoid Losing Your Cool

1. *Get your priorities straight; know what is primary and that which is secondary, and those things that are peripheral to you.*
2. *Lower your annoyance level.*
3. *Rejoice in your healthy self-esteem.*
4. *Avoid jumping to conclusions.*
5. *Remind yourself that God loves you.*

19 God's Handkerchief
Broken Hearts

"The world breaks everyone and afterward many are strong at the broken places."

—Ernest Hemingway

No emotion is so universal or neglected as grief, and none has a greater potential for teaching and maturing. Do you ever feel that while God whispers in joy, He shouts in pain? The problem is: How do we manage to survive when grief comes, and then learn from it.

A friend, one of the most successful professionals I have known—a public school superintendent and university president, said before he died, "My regret is that we've been so busy with church business we've never had time to discuss the things that really matter such as life after death." A plaintive, poignant tone was in his voice, and I remembered John Wesley's sentence: "Christians die well." Do you recall that wonderful statement by a first-century pagan about the first believers? "They bear their dead away rejoicing and singing, as if they were going to a feast." To a pagan world, which hopelessly laid its dead away, it was like springtime after the bitter coldness of winter. For the first believers, death was an immediate reality. Nine out of every ten children died in infancy; thirty-five was thought old and all life was incredibly cheap. We may have delusions of immortality, but they did not.

It was to a young man the apostle Paul wrote long ago of one who had conquered death and "brought life and immortality to light through the gospel" (2 Tim. 1:10). They believed no person has learned to live who has not come to terms with his own mortality, yet they were possessed of a "blessed hope" which made them live on tiptoe. For them, time was infused with eternity, and they possessed here and now "the power of an endless life."

While all this is true, grief is still difficult to bear.

> The bustle in a House
> The morning after Death
> Is the solemnest of industries
> Enacted upon Earth—
>
> The Sweeping up the Heart
> And putting Love away
> We shall not want to use again
> Until Eternity.[1]

The purpose of this chapter, while not exactly "Sweeping up the Heart/And putting Love away," is learning to reroute our love and live joyfully and abundantly again. But don't be deceived, for such is never simple or easy, and often all we can do, at first, is manage to survive.

Our losses, however, are much broader than physical death, as difficult as that is. Life itself is a composite of gains and losses: losses necessary for gains and losses that seem to net no gain. Judith Viorst in her searching book, *Necessary Losses* in the subtitle wrote of "the loves, illusions, dependencies and impossible expectations that all of us have to give up in order to grow." "The losses are a part of life, universal, unavoidable, inexorable." "We grow by losing, leaving, and letting go."[2] Throughout our lives we grow by giving up, and then there is our final leaving, letting go.

Have you been a parent? Perhaps then you can understand better what all this means. The journey from birth to crawling, toddling, standing, and walking is long and painful but only the beginning of an urgent need to become a separate self. When does this *I* become a reality? Only when for the sake of maturity, self-hood, and independence we surrender our past dependences. The child wishes to be free and to hold on to Mother's support at the same time, but complete freedom is possible only when the child lets go. Letting go can be complex and perplexing. In childhood and even adolescence we can dream of many selves, and perhaps to some degree all have a number of contradictory selves dwelling in us most of the time: the playful child, the anxious teenager, the proper parent, and the rebellious youth. We have to learn to live with this reality, learn to focus, unify, and harmonize these selves, find a positive self-esteem, a healthy love of self, and an inner image both realistic and confident.

This giving up—infancy, childhood, adolescence, even youth—is necessary if we are to become autonomous, free, adult, and mature. We must accept the loss of what we cannot keep, mourn until we can let it go, and then move on to a fuller, freer, more useful life. We expect and accept an infant in a crib, but when we find one the head of a corporation, there's bound to be trouble. How was it the apostle Paul put it? "When I was a child, I spoke as a child, I understood as a child, I thought as a child: but when I became a man, I put away childish things" (1 Cor. 13:11). Even love has to do with our losses, putting away "childish things."

This letting go can be painful and exasperating. In the process we need each other, the steadying love of parents, the community of support and care, and the reminder of the joys of autonomy. We must mourn if we are to give up our past and move on. To become adult is to learn we cannot expect special treatment, absolute control, perfect safety, unconditional love, and exemption from pain and loss. We have to give up the parent and *become* the parent. We have to surrender our faith in magic, fairy tales, and lovely dreams. We learn no two people can gratify all of each other's needs. We learn to live in a real world, to take responsibility for our own lives, and to find joy in serving others. Indeed, we live by losing, leaving, and letting go; we gain by giving up.

There are also the losses, which appear to have no net gain, the dark angels of death who take away those we love best: a parent loses a child, a child loses a parent, a spouse loses a spouse, a sibling loses a sibling, a friend loses a friend. Each year in the U.S., four-hundred thousand children die before they reach the age of twenty-five. And while infant mortality continues to decline, there are many stillborns, and the death of young children is widespread. Every year there are eight-hundred thousand new widowers and widows. Which is the most difficult? Who can say? A youth where there is loss of future expectations as well as a shared past? How often I have heard the lament of a parent, "Why didn't I go first?" But there is little profit in grading pain. How do we endure it, learn from it, and overcome it? How do we recover our energy, our optimism, our capacity to enjoy and invest in life?

Sometimes we internalize something about the person we love and have lost: gardening, love of flowers, painting, music, or deeds of kindness. Doing what he or she loved brings us joy. "Holding on to grief" however is not loyalty to a loved one but the reverse. We cannot live in "suspended unreality" without devastating loss. We must mourn. Mourning is the process of adapting to the losses of life. We mourn the loss of others, but we also mourn the loss of ourselves. To deny our grief is the worst way of all, for denied grief multiplies like an infection and spreads its poisons. Our only valid choice is to decide what to do with our dead:

To die when they die,

To live crippled,

Or to move on.

If we are to move on, then it will help if we know the steps in grieving, the process through which most of us go in coming to terms with our loss.

1. *First, there is shock, numbness, and a sense of disbelief.* Perhaps our inability to comprehend fully helps us gain the time necessary to adjust.
2. *Next, there is denial.* What we cannot accept, we deny. Life appears irrational and hopeless.
3. *Then there is anger and guilt.* Death never seems fair, and in such anguish we always wish we could have done more.
4. *Often there is a stage of idealizing or canonizing.* The one who is gone seems to have had no faults, and we need to share this dream.

5. *Then there is depression, despair, and gloom* when we wish we could also die.
6. *Finally, we complete our mourning and begin to move on.*

Sometimes children need special help. There are many variables, of course, but as a rule they need good family relationships, prompt and accurate information about death, an invitation to join in the grieving process, and a comforting caretaker.

We mourn the death of a loved one, the loss of a friend, the failure of a marriage, or a bankruptcy in business. Who can say which is the most painful? Divorced friends say a divorce is both death and rejection, and the completion of mourning can be more difficult.

Our most poignant mourning may be in coming to terms with our own mortality. We spend sixty, seventy, eighty and sometimes ninety years in discovering who we are, what we can do, and why we are here. For what? For dying? That's the reason the pagan world of the first century listened with bated breath to the wonder of the gospel with its promise of eternal life.

> And does it not seem hard to you,
> When all the sky is clear and blue,
> And I should like so much to play,
> To have to go to bed by day.[3]

After a while, we become aware of the deeper meaning of Robert Louis Stevenson's lines.

To live a life in which death is denied is a poor life indeed. If one is not able to die, one is not able to live. Here is beauty, truth, exuberance, agony, and ecstasy. You can accept death calmly and with faith, run away from it, fight against it, or look upon it as the door into a fuller life.

Our losses and our gains are inexorably mixed, but our final gain is in becoming what we were created to be.

See what love the Father has given us, that we should be called children of God; and so we are. The reason why the world does not know us is that it did not know him. Beloved, we are God's children now; it does not yet appear what we shall be, but we know that when he appears we shall be like him, for we shall see him as he is. And every one who thus hopes in him purifies himself as he is pure (1 John 3:1-3, RSV).

Helping in Bereavement:

1. *Don't pretend.*
2. *Let the bereaved grieve.*
3. *Don't fear tears.*
4. *Listen, love, and reassure.*
5. *Do call again.*

20　Here I Stand
Commitment

"Here is the difference . . . I look to men. You
. . . trust everything to God."

—Hutter to Luther

Defying all the powers that be: emperor, pope, the consensus of age, the glory of a vanishing heritage, facing excommunication, and perhaps death, a little Wittenburg monk named Martin Luther, a miner's son with nothing but his own faith and the Word of God to sustain him declared, "Here I stand. I cannot do otherwise. God help me. Amen."[1] By raw courage and strong faith he pointed the church back to the Bible and started the Protestant Reformation.

While our experiences may be less dramatic, all of us, if we are to claim our personhood, must stand on our own feet, make our own choices, and be accountable for our deeds. It is the price of maturity, the essence of individuality, and the sinew of integrity. Neither parent, nor spouse, nor friend can decide for us. Paul Tillich spoke of it as "the courage to be," and it may be the final mark of "the image of God" stamped within us. Perhaps in the beginning, for all of us, our inner monitors are the consciences of our

171

parents, mentors, or friends, but if we are to become what God intended us to be, we must reach the place where our choices are determined by our *own* perception, sense of values, moral stances and faith. We must be able to say, "Here I stand."

Are you sure where you stand?

Every age, even ages which claim otherwise, has its value systems, expressed or unexpressed, recognized or unrecognized, and choices are made on the basis of these presuppositions. We've all committed to something, and we have our absolutes, even if they are only determinations not to have absolutes. We live in the latter years of the "me generation" where we're out to do our thing and prove there are no moral absolutes, but few are free, and even fewer live at peace with themselves. Indulgence, tolerance, open-mindedness, even free and easy—these are our words instead of commitment and discipline. We advocated sex without commitment, and AIDS came along; marriage without commitment, and divorce and misery ensued; education and wealth without commitment, and greed, poverty, and violence plague our society. We're beginning to learn that without discipline there is no freedom; without perseverance, no achievement; without commitment, no abundant life.

There were, no doubt, reasons for the rebellion against absolutes. Rules exist for people, not people for rules. Jesus made this clear. We can only tolerate so much negative, angry judgment, especially from loveless bigots. Only God is absolute; our perception of Him and His rules are always relative, and His one absolute for us is love which characterizes him and His relationship to all creation. But there are values which are absolute in the sense that without them, societies destroy themselves. Do you think of the Ten Commandments, for example, as "God's laws of human happiness"? We do not break them; we break *ourselves* upon them.

What are the values to which we must be committed, the principles on which we can say, "Here I stand"? Here are ten worth remembering, treasuring, and incorporating into your feelings, thoughts, and deeds:

- We were created to love and to be loved.
- We live by truth, not falsehood.
- Without commitment, there can be no intimacy.
- Without constraints, there is no freedom.
- To be free is to be responsible.
- Excellence is always costly.
- Morality carries its own reward.
- The happy life is the useful life.
- Generosity and joy are twins.
- Our deepest hunger is our hunger for God.

If we are to make it through the day (and through the years) undefeated, productive, useful, and at peace with ourselves, the most essential requirement is commitment. To what, to whom, and how are you committed? There are values greater than any person's life. To which of them are you committed? Where do you draw the line? For what do you make the sacrifice?

What do you want most? Money, success in business or a profession, to wield political power, to be acclaimed by others, to have a Christian home and family, be a loving parent, to live a good life, or to be of value to God's kingdom? Your success will be relative to your commitment. The ancient proverb is right, "You take what you want and pay for it." Good or bad, you pay a price, and get what you pay for.

Which of life's commitments is the most important? Who can say? Every part of life is precious, every age, every relationship, even every feeling. Who can say which counts the most in the eyes of God: the laughter of a child, a mother's song, or an old man's tears? Let us consider three as representative: commitment and marriage, commitment and personal integrity, commitment and faith.

Commitment and Marriage

These days the "old-fashioned wedding" is in: Belgium lace veils, white satin gowns with long trains, rows of smartly dressed attendants, church chapels, ministers, and all the trappings. But the Victorian era has not returned nor has permanence in marriage. Nostalgia will not bring it back.

Kate Tyndal of United Press International wrote an article in the August 22, 1987, issue of *The Stars and Stripes* entitled, "Reluctant Marital Partners"[2] which makes poignantly clear that this love of tradition with its whimsical longing for something lost will not restore what is largely gone. Nostalgia cannot substitute for commitment. Sometimes couples explain to ministers how they'd be more comfortable if "until death do us part" could be omitted from the ceremony. When the unconditional nature of Christian marriage is explained to them, they usually agree to the inclusion of the clause, but one wonders with how much mental reservation. They don't even appear to comprehend that conditional commitment can be a self-fulfilling prophecy.

We have seen marriages based on economics and childbearing shift to partnerships based on companionship, pleasure, and convenience. The time-honored illusion of "happily ever after" becomes more and more illusive in today's emotionally-grounded unions. Both women and men are less and less willing to make the sacrifices entailed. "What couples are afraid of," writes Kate Tyndal, "is commitment both to each other and to an institution."[3] They mean to stay together as long as it is mutually convenient, pleasurable, and satisfying. But without commitment, intimacy in marriage soon loses its meaning and may even turn into hatred. Marriage doesn't work—indeed can't work—unless you see it as permanent. Little wonder that 50 percent of today's newlyweds, if the trends follow those of previous decades, will divorce whether their weddings are old-fashioned or contemporary.

Sociologist Jesse Barnard in her classic: *The Future of Marriage* says, "Some kind of commitment must be involved. Without such commitment a marriage may hardly be said to exist at all, even in the most avant-garde patterns."[4] How often I have wished all couples considering marriage could share in depth with all couples and children experiencing divorce. Commitment is costly, but marriage undertaken without it is even costlier.

Commitment and Personal Integrity

The ancient wise one wrote, "Righteousness exhalteth a nation: but sin is a reproach to any people" (Prov. 14:-34). Whose righteousness? The righteousness of the community begins with the righteousness of the individual. Citizens of integrity—men and women who tell the truth, keep their word, respect both the person and property of others, act responsibly, feel compassion, and work for the common good—build stable and righteous communities. However, many factors in modern society tend to erode our sense of personal responsibility. As our common life becomes increasingly mechanized, computerized, and government subsidized, we think of ourselves as less and less responsible. Indeed, we begin to feel helpless and feel that what we do will make little difference.

In addition there is the widespread dishonesty and exploitation in our economic and political life and the lack of evenhanded justice. The cynical feeling that anything goes if you manage not to get caught is prevalent. In such a climate, personal integrity dissipates and may be lost entirely. Yet without personal integrity and commitment, human freedom becomes impossible.

Commitment and Faith

Sholem Asch in his book, *Kiddush Hashem,* told of a young Jewish boy who after the terrible massacre of Jews in Poland in 1648 moved from town to town in search of his family. In Lubin he learned of the death of his parents, and, bewildered, he wandered through the markets filled with refugees. He came upon an old man, crying his wares, but seeing nothing on his shelves, the boy asked, "What do you sell here?" "Faith" was the answer that came back. Bewildered, the youth stood gazing at the old man and slowly began to see in him Abraham, Moses, and Isaiah.

Faith is indeed God's gift, but it is also commitment, choice, and perseverance. Without faith no person can stand for long and standing becomes itself a means for increasing faith. We choose to believe. Strong faith undergirds commitment, and commitment increases faith.

Robert Louis Stevenson, the Scottish writer, once observed, "A man is no use until he has dared everything."
Commit yourself. Here is life's meaning and purpose.

Making Your Commitment Count

1. *Make up your mind about your values.*
2. *Keep the list brief and specific.*
3. *Do something about them every day.*
4. *Be glad God put them in your heart.*

21 The Best Way of All
Love

"To love abundantly is to live abundantly."

—Henry Drummond

In 1939 trainloads of Jewish children, some as young as three years, began rolling into Sweden. The children would file off the trains, thin and pale, with sunken brown eyes; their gaze revealed the suffering they had endured, with no belongings except large identification tags hanging about their necks. Swedish families were taking in the children for "the duration of the war," although most of them knew what that meant. One of the Swedes, a Baptist lathe operator named Johan Eriksson who had been left at twenty-eight a widower with four children, agreed to take a nine-year-old named Roth. Despite all his other responsibilities he could not turn the boy down.

So a small Jewish boy, with nothing but a scarred life, became a member of a Swedish Baptist family. At first, when there was a loud knock at the door, the boy would run and hide in a closet and cover his head paralyzed with fear. Little by little, surrounded by love and trust, he began to gain weight, and eventually to laugh again.

When an invasion of the Nazis seemed imminent, people would say to Johan: "When Hitler comes you will be in trouble with that Jewish boy." The gentle Swede would set his jaws and reply, "They'll never take him so long as I am alive." When members of the church would try to convert the boy, Johan would resist, explaining, "I promised to raise him in the faith of his parents." And he did, seeing that he learned the Jewish traditions and celebrated his bar mitzvah.

When the war was over, Roth's family never returned, having perished in the holocaust. Roth grew up, went away to Stockholm to work, where in time he began to succeed. Then one day, his mind snapped. Perhaps the strain of his youth had been too great. Government officials, believing the young man dangerous, recommended hospitalization, but the gentle Swede would have none of it. "This is his home," he explained. "He belongs here." So Johan took him back to Amal where he nursed him and cared for him until his health returned. Roth returned to Stockholm where he became a successful and wealthy businessman, married, and had a family.

Johan Eriksson's daughter, who emigrated to America, told the above story to Alan Loy McGinnis, her employer. She reported that when her father became ill, Roth would be the first to arrive, and the same was true the day her father died. Her Jewish stepbrother loved his Baptist foster father to the end.[1]

What would motivate a Swedish Baptist lathe operator, a widower with four children, to take in a Jewish refugee and care for him like that? Was it the largeness of his heart? His faith in God? The pain and frustration he had endured caring for his own motherless brood? Was it something a God of infinite love had planted in his soul?

It had to do with what the Bible calls "the greatest of these" (1 Cor. 13:13*b*), and in our better moments we know it is the best way of all. To love abundantly is to live abundantly.

Life has many joys and pains, and most of us are aware of them. What has brought you the greatest joy? What has caused you the most pain? The answer is found in our human relationships. We cannot successfully live alone. We were meant for community. To live a life of loving relationships is to live joyfully, creatively, and abundantly.

Everybody wants to be loved: the helpless infant, the growing child, the aggressive young adult, the ambitious middle ager, and the lonely aged. Some try to manipulate it, some endeavor to purchase it, and some press so hard they strangle it. But love cannot be compelled, purchased, or demanded. Love must be given, shared, learned, and received. Love is a gift, first from God, then from other human beings, nourished in community, and sustained by faith. We seek love at least from the moment of birth and perhaps before. In the nineteenth century there was a period when more than half of all infants died. Indeed, in children's homes the figure was much higher. They died of a disease called *narasmus* (a Greek word meaning "wasting away"). The cause of this tragic phenomenon was a widely read book by a Columbia University professor of pediatrics, which recommended infants be kept isolated, sterile, safe in wards away from human contact, fed on rigid schedules, and not taken up when they cried. Here is an instance of our science overriding our instincts and causing havoc.

Dr. Henry Chafin in his monumental studies of the causes of death in young children had women brought in to feed, clothe, fondle, cradle, and love infants in children's homes, and the dying came to an end. One wonders how many thousands died because of our arbitrary science, so called. There has even been found a direct relationship between physical contact given a child by parents and the child's IQ. To be loved, fondled, and cared for from birth makes healthier, happier, and brighter children. There are reports on a group of young medical interns who, on going to work in a large, East coast pediatric hospital, discovered wide variations in the rate of healing among the children. Soon it became apparent that the children cared for by one young doctor made more rapid recovery than the others. Upon investigation, the discovery was made that the only difference in his care was that he kissed each child good night. The Bible reports that Jesus took young children in His arms and blessed them (Mark 10:16). The "laying on of hands" is an ancient and significant rite of the church. Touch is an important part of love. But listening, sensing, and understanding are also parts of love.

Do you feel you not only love your kids but show your love by word and deed, yet they do not return your love? You may be right, for children cannot love parents like parents love children. But that is part of parental love. Biblical love, *agape,* has to do with "invincible good will," responding to others in God's way, choosing to see people through the eyes of Christ. All of us need to be loved, but demanding or complaining about it will never bring it. If we were loved as children it is easier, but we begin by choosing the life-style of love.

Why do some people draw others to them, make friends, and achieve intimacy with such *apparent* ease?

(Don't overlook the word *apparent,* for as Katherine Anne Porter put it: "Love must be learned, and learned again and again; there is no end to it. Hate needs no instruction, but wants only to be provoked.[2]) Do you want to be loved, then work at making yourself loveable; but even more, work at expressing your love for others, for love produces love.

- *People who are loved believe people and relationships are important.*
- *People who are loved learn to be open and honest—transparent.* They wear fewer masks, play fewer games, and admit their faults and failures. Inhibitions disappear when we are honest with each other.
- *People who are loved are patient, considerate, positive, and hopeful.* They search for goodness in others and expose it. Our opinions of people depend less on what we see in them than upon what they see in us.
- *People who are loved talk about their affections, practice the gestures of love, and work at communication.*
- *People who are loved create space in their relationships.* They know the difference between love and manipulation. To truly love is to enlarge the freedom of the one loved. To love a child is to take pleasure in his or her growth, and growth entails ever enlarging freedom.

There is also a word of warning: It is "always" possible to love but to receive no love in return. Perhaps this is why so many never take the risk. Yet to love is to live, and the life of love carries its own reward. Yet to prevent the pain of "saying good-bye" there are those who never say "hello." Nonetheless, friendship is the springboard of love.

Have you experienced the pain of divorce? "Our marriage died, but there was more. I was rejected, left all alone with a brood of children and inadequate support." That's the way a friend put it once. Or perhaps the person you love most has never responded to your love, or your children appear to reject your love. Remember, you are precious in the heart of a God of love, who loved you even when you rejected His love. Take your pain to Him; leave your anger at the cross; build new relationships. Reject self-pity and resentment as not worth the price they exact from your joy and peace of mind.

Let me give you what I call "My Laws of Love." Live by them. Cherish them. Make them keys to a life of joy.

1. *Begin by accepting God's love for you.* You don't deserve it. You can't merit it or even comprehend it. But that has no effect on His grace. He loves you all the same and awaits your response of faith. His is the love that will not let you go, the source and ground of your love. You cannot prove His love, but you cannot live without it. When you accept God's love, you are prepared for step number two.

2. *You make up your mind to love yourself.* I cannot tell you why this is so difficult, but I know it is. Why do we find it easier to condemn ourselves, berate ourselves, and punish ourselves rather than forgive ourselves? It is a strange mystery of our human ways. Perhaps it has to do with our pride in wishing to pay for our sins when we cannot do so. I do not know. But I do know we cannot hate ourselves—made in the image of God who loves us—without at the same time rejecting God's love. Jesus commanded us to love our neighbor as ourselves.

Make a list of what it would mean in your life if you really loved yourself. To love yourself is to fight for your own uniqueness, to be open to your potential, to accept the love of others at face value, to take seriously the reality of your better self, to reward yourself as well as blame yourself, and to be glad God made you as you are.

3. *Love is the source of love and can only be learned in community.* Books and theories and clever abstractions won't do it. Love is taught, like language and walking, by modeling. Parents who love each other and their children teach those children to love.

4. *God is the measure of love, not love of God.* Love, in our age, means everything and nothing, all the way from sacrifices to lust. In our time it has become an obsession, a match made for the young, an excuse for the permissive, and a cliché for the religious. We speak of loving a world we don't even want to know and somehow imagine we can love without paying the price of intimacy. Our only antidote to such foolishness is to remember "God is love" and to see that love in light of the cross. To live the life of love is to be willing to pay any price for the redemption of all life. Here is the secret and source of our being, our life, and our joy.

5. *For us, love is choice.* We choose to love God. Perhaps, at times it seems easier to hate Him, and the circumstances of our days may seem to conspire to prove Him unloving. There were times when Hitler seemed more powerful than Dietrich Bonhoeffer and Ayatollah Khomeini more significant than Mother Teresa. But while love may lead to the cross, only love can redeem. We choose to love God, each other, our neighbors, our

enemies, and a needy world. The best way of all, it is rarely the easiest. But love is the way of God: the way of life.

What is the reward of love? Is it that only by loving we are able to love? Perhaps a better answer is that love is the law of our being. Aristotle understood that the happiness of any creature depends on its being what it was meant to be.

There's a beautiful story about a public school teacher who abruptly became aware one morning that there were two boys in her class with the same last name. Asking one if they were brothers, she received this reply: "Yes, but one of us is adopted, and I can't remember which one it is." All day long the teacher thought about a home where parents could rear an adopted and a natural child in such a manner that they wouldn't be aware of which was adopted.

Making Love Work Every Day

1. *Love is something you do.*
2. *To start with judgment is to make love impossible.*
3. *Love begins with patience and grows with gratitude.*
4. *Only love lasts forever.*

Epilogue

If you've come to this page, you've made it both through your day and this book. I'm glad. People read books in many ways. Sometimes they begin and later give up. Sometimes they pick and choose. If the book is an exciting novel or an intriguing mystery, they may read right through for joy or to satisfy curiosity. Regardless of how you have read this book, I am glad.

Perhaps now, I can share with you the convictions that underlie these pages. For me, the book is not another self-help manual in the "faith-for-faith's-sake" genre; it is not another brief for positive thinking. There is grotesque evil in the world and frightful pain, and so often the best seem to suffer the most. But despite all these inequities, I believe this is a good world created by a God of love who is working in your life and mine His benevolent purposes.

"Life can only be understood backwards," once observed Soren Kirkegaard. Then he added, "but it must be lived forward." In my youth I was so obsessed with changing my circumstances, I gave little consideration to the choices we live by. I was taught to compete, achieve, and succeed rather than to enjoy, experience, and celebrate. The heart indeed has reasons the mind knows not of, but

I spent many years learning the truth. All of us make our choices and live by them. These are mine:

I choose to believe, despite all evidence to the contrary, that this is a good world and one day God will balance the scales. I believe love is stronger than hate, goodness is stronger than evil, faith is stronger than doubt, and life is stronger than death.

I choose to believe God is love, and that His love lies behind every good thing in this mysterious, miraculous universe. To me "original goodness" is equally significant with "original sin," for God's love sets us free to be what He intended us to be.

Finally, I choose to believe love is the purpose of our life on earth. With Goethe I'm convinced, "Life is the childhood of eternity" where love endures forever. Is it too much to pray that "Someday after we have mastered the wind, the waves, the tide and gravity, we will harness the energy of love"? If we do, "then for the second time man will have discovered fire."[1]

My prayer for you, in the words of Jonathan Swift, is: "May you live all the days of your life."

Notes

Chapter 1

1. Festus, Philip James Bosley, n.d., n.p., n.p.n.
2. Meditations, Book II, *Familiar Quotations,* ed. John Bartlett (Boston: Little, Brown and Co., 1980), p. 124.
3. Source unavailable.

Chapter 2

1. Alan Loy McGinnis, *The Friendship Factor* (Minneapolis: Augsburg, 1987). n.p.n. My list is somewhat modified from McGinnis's, but I commend his book for its honesty, practicality, and hopefulness.
2. Ibid., p. 114-115.

Chapter 3

1. My student kindly granted permission to use the report of his experience.
2. Vol. 28, No. 6, p.1.
3. Ibid., p. 10.

Chapter 4

1. Terri Schultz, *Bittersweet: Surviving and Growing from Loneliness* (New York: Thomas Y. Crowell Co., 1976), n.p.n.
2. Ibid., p. 13.
3. Ralph Keyes, *We, the Lonely People: in Order to Form a More Perfect Community* (New York: Harper and Row, 1973), p. 45.
4. Schultz, p. 109.
5. Velma Darbo Stevens, *A Fresh Look at Loneliness* (Nashville: Broadman Press, 1981), p. 29.

Chapter 5

1. William Manchester, *The Last Lion: Winston Churchill, Visions of Glory* (Boston: Little, Brown Co., 1983), p. 7.

Chapter 6

1. From *Executive Health.* Vol. XIX, No. 5, Feb. 1983. P. O. Box 589, Rancho Santa Fe, Calif. 92067, p. 1.

2. Ibid., p. 3.

Chapter 7

1. Note: Eric Fromm, *For the Love of Life.* (New York: The Free Press, 1986).

2. Alan Loy McGinnis, *Bringing Out the Best in People* (Minneapolis: Augsburg, 1985), p. 22.

3. Ibid., p. 126 *ff.*

4. Rabbi Harold S. Kushner, *When All You've Ever Wanted Isn't Enough* (New York: Summit Books, 1965), p. 1 *ff.*

5. Ibid., p. 82.

Chapter 8

1. Julia H. (pseudonym), *Letting Go with Love* (Los Angeles: Jeremy P. Tarcher, Inc., 1987), n.p.n.

2. Arthur H. Cain, *Young People and Drugs* (New York: The John Day Company, 1969), p. 33.

3. Stephen Arter-burn, *Growing Up Addicted,* (New York: Ballentine Books, 1987), p. 3.

4. Ruth Maxwell, *Breakthrough: What to Do When Chemical Dependency Hits Home.* (New York: Ballentine Books, 1986), pp. 3-4.

5. Maxwell, *Breakthrough,* p. 238.

Chapter 10

1. Robert L. Woolfolk and Frank C. Richardson, *Stress, Sanity, and Survival* (New York: A Sovereign Book by Monarch, 1978), p. 51 *ff.*

2. Ibid., p. 62 *ff.*

Chapter 12

1. Kathleen H. Bernhard, *Jealousy: Its Nature and Treatment* (Springfield, Il: Charles C. Thomas, 1986), p. 23.

Chapter 15

1. Judith Viorst, *Necessary Losses.* (New York: Fawcett Gold Medal, 1986), p. 97.

2. Ibid., p. 227-228.

3. Dr. Kenneth Chafin.

Chapter 16

1. Robert L. Woolfolk and Frank C. Richardson, *Stress, Sanity, and Survival* (New York: A Sovereign Book published by Monarch, 1978), p. 31 *ff.*

Chapter 18

1. Alan Loy McGinnis, *Bringing Out the Best in People* (Minneapolis: Augsburg, 1985), p. 72.

2. McGinnis, *The Friendship Factor,* (Minneapolis: Augsburg, 1987), p. 30.

Chapter 19

1. Emily Dickinson, *The Complete Poems,* ed. by Thomas H. Johnson (Boston: Little, Brown & Co., 1960), p. 489.

2. Judith Viorst, *Necessary Losses* (New York: Fawcett Gold Medal, 1986), p. 3 *ff.*

3. "Bed in Summer," Robert Louis Stevenson from *Underwoods Works of Robert Louis Stevenson.*

Chapter 20

1. Roland H. Bainton, *Here I Stand: A Life of Martin Luther* (New York: Abingdon-Cokesbury, 1950), p. 386.

2. Kate Tyndal, *"Reluctant Marital Patterns,"* *Stars and Stripes,* 22 Aug. 1987, p. 17.

3. Ibid.

4. Jesse Barnard, *The Future of Marriage* (New York: World), p. 79.

Chapter 21

1. Alan Loy McGinnis, *Bringing Out the Best in People* (Minneapolis: Augsburg, 1985), p. 174. (Eriksson's daughter who came to live in U.S. related the story to McGinnis).

2. Alan Loy McGinnis, *The Friendship Factor* (Minneapolis: Augsburg, 1987), p. 20.

Epilogue

1. Teilhard de Chardin, *Pierre* (New York: Harper & Row, 1972), p. 33 *ff.*